karmic Healing

Clearing Past Life Blocks
to Present Day Love,
Health, and Happiness

djuna wojton

CROSSING PRESS
Berkeley | Toronto

Disclaimer

Past-life therapy is not a substitute for medical or psychiatric care. The process is challenging work, best accomplished by those who are emotionally and physically well balanced. Seek appropriate medical help if you have a medical problem. If you are currently in therapy, consult with your therapist before investigating past lives.

If you have suffered emotional, physical, or sexual abuse in your childhood, *please* seek out professional support with a qualified therapist in healing the trauma before exploring past-life hypnotic regression. People who have experienced childhood abuse need to clear away suppressed feelings of grief and rage. They also need a support system to process such intense emotions before they can delve into their past lives.

All of the names of the clients mentioned in this book have been changed to protect their privacy.

Crossing Press
A Division of Ten Speed Press
PO Box 7123
Berkeley, California 94707

Distributed in Australia by Simon and Schuster Australia, in Canada by Ten Speed Press Canada, in New Zealand by Southern Publishers Group, in South Africa by Real Books, and in the United Kingdom and Europe by Airlift Book Company.

Cover design Lisa Buckley
Interior design by Michael Cutter

ISBN-13: 978-1-58091-178-8

Printed the United States of America

Dedication

This book is dedicated to my husband, Bruce, for his calming presence, love, and unconditional support.

contents

acknowledgments

I want to thank everyone who has contributed to this book. There have been so many. I could not have accomplished writing *Karmic Healing* without the support of my community.

First, I'd like to thank my clients and students for the honor and privilege of being part of your healing process and transformation. I want to acknowledge your generosity in sharing your stories so that others may heal.

I am grateful for all of my teachers (living and in spirit) who have passed their knowledge to me, so that I may serve humanity. Thanks to Sheila Reynolds, Sandra Stevens, and Evelyn Isador for initiating me into past life regression. I give special thanks to Tish and Joel Pacman for the teachings of the flowers. I also express deep gratitude to all of the flowers and their healing essences.

I'd like to thank my agent, Diane Gedymin, for your commitment to this book. I am very grateful for all of your expertise and guidance and for having faith in me.

I'd like to thank all at Crossing Press, especially Jo Ann Deck and my editors, Shirley Coe, Carrie Rodrigues, and Brie Mazurek for your excellence. I'd also like to thank Lisa Buckley for her cover design and Michael Cutter for his book design.

Many thanks to friends who have been involved in the process of writing this book. I appreciate that you took time out of your busy schedules to read and offer creative input on the work. You were always there when I needed you, lending encouragement or editorial expertise. Your faith in this work empowered me to go beyond what I thought I could do. Special thanks to M. L. Polak, Lucartha Kohler, Brigitta Herrmann, Dr. Elliot Diamond, Susan Gale, and Deborah Hoffman. Helen Shonbrun was also invaluable in helping me with the book proposal and initial chapters.

I wish to thank those who helped the book when it was a seedling, especially Natalie Shapiro for editing during your baby's naptime, and Marcella Landres for your encouragement.

I have deep appreciation for those who nurtured me through the process of creating this book. Thank you to my husband, Bruce Pollock; my reiki group; my massage therapist, Kaye Seger; Monteo Myers for your healing stones; my Feldenkrais practitioner, Joe Ankenbrand; and my acupuncturist, Dr. Cheng-hui Zhu.

I'd also like to thank my community at Landmark Education, who taught me to be unstoppable when the going gets tough.

And most of all, I am very grateful for my parents, Stanley and Stella Wojton, for propelling me on my karmic healing journey.

introduction
Delving into the Unknown

You want your life to have meaning. Perhaps you sometimes wonder, "Do I have a reason for being here on Earth?" Or maybe life has been so challenging you find yourself asking, "I am a good person, so why is my life so hard?" How can this book benefit you? Using the karmic healing techniques I present here—which I've developed over the years in my practice—have helped many people find answers to such questions. If you apply what you learn from this book, you will find similar answers and also experience a deeper sense of purpose and more fulfilling relationships. You will feel more relaxed and empowered to meet life's challenges.

Past-life regression is one karmic healing technique I use with clients. When I ask workshop participants to share what they want to get out of experiencing a past-life regression, most usually don't know. In fact, most say, "I am not even sure that I really *believe* in past lives. I'm just curious to see what will happen." When they delve into the unknown and engage in the process, they discover something new about themselves. The experience can range from being merely interesting to being highly profound.

I've witnessed a myriad of past-life journeys over the past two decades, and each person's experience was unique. The stories in this book are based on the real experiences of my clients. Although I've documented their past-life stories and followed up on their progress over the years, I've never felt the need to research whether the stories had historical validity. Because clients had healings, emotional releases, and profound insights, proving people's stories seemed irrelevant. You can accept the philosophy of reincarnation or reject it, but we may never be able to prove it to be true.

What I do have evidence of, however, is that the process of past-life regression produces positive changes in people's lives. When people are regressed to a past life, the story that emerges can be seen as a metaphor for internal conflicts. The core issue or problem is revealed and, by rising to the surface, can be healed.

Even in a normal state of consciousness, the art of story-telling is very powerful; that's why movies and novels are so popular. When we involve ourselves with certain fictional characters and situations, it helps us heal parts of ourselves that have been wounded or lost.

Although people struggle with common issues, I've never heard the same story twice. I can assure skeptics that I've never encountered such famous figures as Cleopatra or Napoleon. Retrieving past-life information is not meant to glorify your personality or boost your ego. Rather, its benefit occurs when you receive insights, have a cathartic emotional release, or are healed in some way.

What I find most interesting is this: while the characters in past-life stories are, indeed, ordinary people, the dramas they enact are extraordinary. The stories people share range from humdrum vignettes to detailed sagas.

Regression experiences fall into one or more of these five categories:

- You experience another lifetime as a complete story.
- You briefly glimpse a series of visual images accompanied by a flash of spiritual insight and a deep sense of well-being.
- You experience pain or uncomfortable body sensations that disappear when you return to a normal waking state. These pains are often related to chronic health ailments. Sometimes the ailments clear up after the regression.

- You release your fear, anger, or grief.
- You feel so peaceful and relaxed that you don't want to come out of trance. When you do return to normal waking consciousness, you feel refreshed and revitalized.

People don't always explore past-life regression just because they are curious. Those who come to me for a private karmic healing session are usually dealing with one of the following issues:

- **In crisis:** Having suffered a loss of some kind, perhaps a death or divorce, they need spiritual comfort.
- **Blocked:** Mired in guilt, confusion, or fear, they either don't know what they want or can't achieve their goals.
- **Struggling:** Entrenched in high drama, they are entangled in a difficult relationship.
- **Inquisitive:** Eager for growth and development, they want to "know themselves."

Unresolved past-life memories can block our aura or individual energy field, impeding the free flow of energy and limiting our experience of the world. Even the satisfaction we receive from our relationships becomes impaired. These blockages may weaken the state of our health.

What makes regression and healing possible is this: the world of our subconscious is far greater than the world that our conscious mind inhabits. Our subconscious is holistically connected to our soul. When we access our soul, we heal at the deepest level of our being.

Often when people are in a growth period, they need support while undergoing changes. During a past-life regression session, I create a safe, nurturing space for clients so they can go within and connect with their inner self. I act as a guide while they chart new territory. As a result of experiencing a past-life regression, people tend to:

- find inner peace
- dissolve inner barriers, gain clarity, and achieve their goals
- release destructive emotional patterns and self-defeating attitudes, thereby improving their relationships
- connect to their soul, align with their purpose, and release any fears of death

The karmic healing process can help you understand the spiritual lesson behind the challenges you are facing. You'll be able to see the bigger picture. You will receive insights about why you are going through a difficult set of circumstances, and then you will be empowered to meet them with strength.

My Own Karmic Journey

I began investigating my own past lives back in the 1980s because I was an emotional wreck and needed guidance. During my twenties and early thirties, I suffered the loss of most of my close family members. My father died unexpectedly of a stroke when he was only fifty-six years old. Within a relatively short period of time, six of my nine aunts and uncles passed into Spirit. Then I lost my mother and grandparents.

I was grief stricken and lonely. After attending funeral after funeral, I wondered whether there was a larger purpose to it all. Was all life empty and meaningless? I felt there *had* to be more. My quest to find an answer drew me to study metaphysics, which led me to the concepts of karma and reincarnation. I joined a school that taught the connections between the tarot, Kabbalism, and astrology. I began to study yoga as well.

When Mind Matters, a psychic and spiritual development center, offered a past-life workshop, I eagerly registered. Waiting for the regression program to begin, lying on my mat on the floor, I was filled with conflicting emotions. One moment I wondered whether I had been someone famous. The next I feared I would learn I had done something horrible. I was so nervous I wasn't sure I'd be able to relax. What I finally discovered was neither glamorous nor frightening.

The lights were lowered, and my teacher began speaking in a slow, nearly monotonous voice. Soft music played in the background. As I drifted into trance, I was surprised by what I experienced. I saw an image in my mind's eye of a dark-haired man standing at an easel, painting a vase of flowers. I knew he—I— was independently wealthy and had devoted his (my) life to art.

As I was guided to view my death, another image of that man, now lying on a bed, flashed into my mind's eye. Suddenly I felt as if I were floating. I felt light and free. An all-encompassing sense of love permeated my entire being. I felt as though I didn't have a physical body, and my unencumbered spirit reached all the way up to the stars. In that moment I knew I was not my body; I was not the personality known as Djuna. I was part of everyone and everything. I was filled with light.

In that state of peace and clarity I began to review the losses I'd experienced in my present life. I had a revelation. "What if my soul had chosen the circumstances of this lifetime in order to motivate me to seek a spiritual path now?" Perhaps in my previous lives I was often content to float along in shallow water, with no real need to probe the deeper meaning of life.

I asked my inner self why that specific artist's life was revealed to me. All of a sudden the answer occurred: as a child I had been labeled "gifted." I have a natural talent for drawing. By the time I graduated from high school, I had won many awards and received a scholarship to the Cleveland Institute of Art. I had always wondered where this came from since there were no artists in my ancestral tree. Now I knew that my talent was a true gift from Spirit.

I had never felt such a state of peace and well-being as during my regression. The whole experience was so profound that I vowed to share the process with others. I went on to become a certified hypnotherapist and reiki master. I also became certified in other healing modalities such as herbal medicine and shamanism. Throughout this time I explored a variety of holistic therapies for my own growth.

As a result I began to undergo many personal changes. My anxiety dissolved and left me with a sense of inner peace, and my ability to concentrate expanded. My fearfulness turned into confidence. I began to do things I never dreamed I could do, ranging from speaking in front of large groups of people to ocean kayaking in the Pacific.

The way I viewed my losses also shifted. I ultimately saw those hard lessons as a great gift. I certainly learned how to let go. I also learned that the relationships we have are precious and won't last forever. The essence of life is change.

Your Spiritual Path

To those who are new on the spiritual path, past-life regression may seem confusing or bewildering at first. Many people fear they may just "make up something." They are afraid they won't have an authentic experience. It takes time and patience to learn the symbolic language of your soul and to trust your psychic impressions.

In workshops, I find a person's level of psychic and spiritual development affects their results. Those who are skilled at focusing and relaxing are better able to access their subconscious and thereby have transformational experiences. However, it's a skill that can be learned like anything else. And I will teach you how.

Whether you believe past lives exist or not doesn't affect your ability to access your subconscious mind. I like to compare past-life regression with dream interpretation because both processes use the subconscious to access soul wisdom. When you go to sleep, you enter the world of dreams. You can have wild adventures, feel intense emotions, and receive inner guidance. The same is true when you enter a trance state and are guided into the realm of past lives. Plus, you always remember your journey when you awaken.

The details of the journey aren't important. Or even whether a memory is *true*. What is important is the content of the experience. The spiritual message or the healing you receive is the true gift of this work.

Yoga's Role in Karmic Healing

Practicing yoga reminds me again and again that humans are energy beings. Our subconscious thoughts, belief systems, and feelings are energetically connected throughout our whole body, impacting the way we act, move, or position our bodies, even influencing our state of health. Western medicine is catching up with this idea and has recognized that stress can affect one's physical well-being.

Yoga is so much more than twisting your body into pretzel-like poses. Whenever we practice relaxation, self-hypnosis, visualization, and meditation, we are using yoga techniques. These techniques are thousands of years old. They are designed to awaken our soul's awareness, both eternal and divine, and can help us know our true purpose in this life.

Yoga provides many benefits:

- It helps you stay calm.
- It strengthens your intuitive abilities.
- It enhances your ability to concentrate.
- It helps you hear your inner voice so you don't need to rely on others for advice.

The systems of body and mind work together holistically—a past-life pattern usually has an emotional, a mental, and a physical component. During a past-life regression, people experience the pattern through one or more of these channels.

Seeking Karmic Healing

I've worked with many people who have endured difficult life circumstances. While they might not uncover a past life during a healing session, they do discover this lifetime's karmic lesson, which aids their healing. Their lives are then blessed by a sense of peace they have never felt before.

Sharon was a participant in one of my past-life classes at a university in Philadelphia. Heartbroken, she enrolled in the course because she was seeking consolation. Kenny, her fiancé, whom she'd believed to be her soul mate, had died recently in a car accident.

Sharon was so distraught over her loss that I suggested she have private sessions with me. The story of her whirlwind romance is what I term a "karmic red flag," which I describe in greater detail in chapter 8.

Sharon was divorced with two kids and had a lousy relationship with her ex-husband. She dated for four years after her divorce, but couldn't find Mr. Right. She was about to give up on men when a friend introduced her to Kenny. The moment they set eyes on each other they knew they were entwined by destiny. She was so nervous and excited, she felt like a teenager.

They spent their first date dancing together passionately; they were like magnets that could not be separated. Every night of the following week, they talked and laughed on the phone until dawn. Five days later Kenny said, "I love you. I want to marry you and live the rest of our lives together."

Sharon was thrilled to meet his parents, who welcomed her into their family.

She felt as if she were dreaming—it all seemed too good to be true. She kept saying, "Somebody pinch me!" They were in love and inseparable. He was a terrific lover, and her exciting new sex life was beyond anything she had experienced with her ex-husband. The feelings of love they shared were so strong they seemed overpowering.

After four weeks of spending a magical time with Kenny, Sharon's dream turned into a nightmare. While dining at a romantic restaurant, Kenny unexpectedly started popping pills and drinking vodka. His personality dramatically changed from a Dr. Jekyll to a Mr. Hyde. One minute Kenny was funny and charming, and the next he was nasty and belligerent. Toward the end of dinner he passed out.

Sharon was alarmed and confused. Right after she dropped Kenny off at his apartment, she phoned his mother. His mother broke the news. Kenny was a recovering alcoholic, and apparently he had fallen off the wagon. She also warned Sharon that Kenny could be violent. He had beaten up his previous girlfriend while in a drunken rage. Kenny's mother promised that she would take him to a rehabilitation center. However, he never got there. The next morning Kenny died in a car accident.

The Four Principles of Karmic Healing

Although Sharon never recalled an actual past life that she had shared with Kenny, our healing sessions greatly helped her resolve his death. She applied the four principles of karmic healing:

- **Responsibility:** Be accountable for your actions. You can't control your circumstances or the reactions of others, but you can master your responses to life.

- **Recognition:** Understand that all of your challenges are opportunities for growth and development.
- **Reason:** Accept that people are in your life for a purpose.
- **Forgiveness:** Forgive mistakes and transgressions. This will help you release anger and resentment toward yourself and others.

Sharon took responsibility for her part in the relationship. She realized that marrying Kenny would have been a disaster. Getting involved with him too deeply and too quickly was reckless. When the soul yearns for healing, we are easily overwhelmed by our feelings. It's typical to be irrational and make hasty choices.

Kenny came into Sharon's life for a reason. She realized Kenny's love for her had touched her soul. It was the first time she had experienced such a powerful feeling. Before she met Kenny, she was trapped in the rat race of the business world. She had never thought about spirituality, the afterlife, or her life's purpose.

Sharon recognized that Kenny's death was a catalyst for her spiritual growth. She was in so much pain that she sought help. She was ready and willing to make some changes in her life. After a few healing sessions, Sharon made peace with Kenny's passing and learned what was most important to her—love.

Our sessions motivated her to transform two important relationships. The first was with her ex-husband. They were not on speaking terms even though they shared parenting responsibilities for their two children. The second was with her mother. They ran a successful retail business and fought every minute they were together.

Sharon stopped blaming her ex and her mother for everything that was wrong and forgave them for past hurts. A year later, I was happy to attend a birthday party at Sharon's home and meet her new lover. Her whole family was there, even her ex, and they were all having a terrific time together.

Throughout this book, you will be guided to heal and resolve relationships with family members, bosses, and romantic partners using the four simple **karmic healing principles** combined with the four-step **karmic healing process**, which I will introduce shortly.

Karma and Reincarnation

I have attended numerous workshops and ceremonies of Buddhist, Hindu, and Earth-based religious traditions, which accept reincarnation as part of their religious doctrine. I personally believe in reincarnation, but you do not have to accept it as part of your worldview to get results from the karmic healing process.

Before we begin to explore some of the ways past lives may be influencing you in the present, we should look at the meaning of karma and reincarnation.

Reincarnation is the process by which our soul passes through different lives on the earth plane to experience life and learn. Each lifetime offers new opportunities to grow in different ways, but ultimately you are here to discover your true self—your spiritual nature—and achieve enlightenment. Your mission is to heal, evolve, and love.

When you explore past lives, sometimes you will find yourself in a male body, sometimes in a female body. You'll live in different countries and be in different social classes. You may be surprised to have a different ethnic background or be a different race.

The Sanskrit word _karma_ literally means "action, activity, or work." It is not synonymous with fate, which is regarded as an inevitable consequence or a ruinous outcome. Nor is it the same as Nemesis (the Greek god of retributive justice), punishment that is deserved.

You have no control of your circumstances, but you do control how you deal with them. Moreover, you are always responsible for your actions. And clearly, you cannot avoid karma because life is composed of action, and action creates karma.

Karma is accumulated throughout lifetimes. It is the amassed consequences of everything you have done in the past, your mistakes as well as your triumphs. Your positive actions have constructive consequences, and your negative actions have destructive consequences. Your karma can be viewed as the result of your past actions that allow you to go forward combined with those that hold you back.

For example, if you are very successful, wealthy, educated, or happy you can conclude from your current good fortune that you are reaping rewards from previous actions. It is likely that in some incarnation you were prudent, diligent, studious, and/or kind. What you choose to do with your current circumstances is another question.

As you know, not every successful person uses his or her assets and advantages productively. How many celebrities who seem to have everything—glamour, wealth, admirers, and fame—end their lives in disaster?

Creating positive karma is like cultivating a garden. You can grow whatever you plant. Your seeds will determine your harvest. If you want fresh corn, then don't scatter pumpkin seeds. In other words, if you want love, act lovingly. What you sow, you will reap.

The Four-Step Karmic Healing Process

You determine the choices you make in life. *Karmic Healing* proposes that you be responsible for those choices. The karmic healing process can be summed up in four easy steps:

- **Retrieve:** Pinpoint your karmic issues by answering specific questions.
- **Remember:** Recall your past-life data by practicing regression meditation.

- **Reprogram:** Use visualizations and affirmations to release negative patterns and imprint new positive images into your mind. Let go of blocks and barriers by using meditations, collage, rituals, writing, or drawings.
- **Reinforce:** Take particular flower essences to reinforce your new attitudes and behaviors.

To see how karmic healing works, let's look at Sarah's case. Sarah had it all—beauty, talent, and wealth. However, she lacked motivation to pursue her career as a vocal artist. She came to my office for a reading because she felt blocked.

Step One—Retrieve: After answering a few simple questions, Sarah pinpointed her main issues. Smoking cigarettes was bad for her voice, but she couldn't seem to quit. She also noticed that her relationship with her boyfriend was out of balance. She was always giving, and he was always taking.

Step Two—Remember: During Sarah's session I suggested that she try a past-life regression to release her block. As Sarah drifted into trance, an image of a powdered wig came to her. Immediately she knew that she was a slave and that her current boyfriend was her master.

She laughed and said, "That's precisely the way I feel now—like a slave to him."

A moment later, Sarah began to cry. "I feel so powerless."

I asked her where she felt the sensation of powerlessness in her body.

"I feel a heaviness and pain in my lower back," she replied.

I asked her to give the feeling an image.

"It feels like a giant block of ice."

"How do you want to remove it?" I asked.

She visualized melting the ice with an imaginary blowtorch. Upon doing so, she released the trapped memory of feeling powerless, still present in her body's subconscious memory. She then filled the space with clear light. She affirmed that she was free to be powerful and to express herself.

When she came out of trance, Sarah was amazed. "I feel so light. I feel like singing," she exclaimed.

We agreed that that was the perfect affirmation for her. She would repeat this positive thought while taking flower essences over the next month.

Step Three—Reprogram: Sarah kicked her cigarette habit when she used collage as a healing tool as part of her homework. She cut and pasted images together to make horrifying scenes that represented what smoking did to her voice. After a few months, and four collages, she was able to quit smoking. As for her relationship, Sarah decided to go into therapy to learn how to stand her ground.

Step Four—Reinforce: During the month following her session, Sarah took a buttercup flower essence to reinforce her affirmation "I feel like singing" and to restore her faith in herself as a vocal artist. A few weeks later, she called to say she was making a promotional video and was busy scheduling performances.

Like Sarah, when you follow these easy steps outlined in *Karmic Healing,* you will:

- **Retrieve** your issues by answering questions
- **Remember** soul wisdom by recalling a past life
- **Reprogram** blocks through a variety of exercises and different types of karmic tools
- **Reinforce** your new life by affirming possibility with flower essences

Your Karmic Toolbox

Throughout this book you'll find meditations and exercises to help you uncover past lives and important karmic issues. You may want to note additional teachings that seem relevant or have special resonance for you. It's best to write down your discoveries so you can refer to them at a later date. Writing down your impressions also helps you interpret the information that is being transmitted to you. Sometimes the data doesn't make sense when you begin to explore past lives, but it will become clear later as you continue your exploration process.

Throughout the exercises in the following chapters, you may notice that personal symbols or images seem to repeat over and over again. Be sure to include these in your journal as collages, pictures cut out from magazines, or perhaps even drawings. Choose a journal that is large enough to hold a variety of media. Even in our age of computers, you may find you prefer a personal journal that you can hold onto and carry with you.

Consider the following when choosing a journal:

- Are you going to write by hand or type?
- Do you want a loose-leaf or a bound book?
- Make sure it is at least 8½ x 11 inches and unlined.
- Take a trip to the art supply store to get some materials that will stimulate your creativity: colored markers, quills, stickers, fanciful pens and ink, or pencils.

Keep the following items on hand as you work with this book:

- old magazines
- scissors, glue, Scotch tape
- photos of people, places, or things that resonate with you
- bits of fabric, lace, or textured paper
- a tape recorder and blank cassettes
- a deck of Rider-Waite tarot cards
- a single terminated (clear) quartz crystal (unless you already have a special stone you use to enhance meditation and trance journeying)
- relaxing music

Tarot cards will be used to enhance your ability to visualize and develop your intuition. You'll learn to interact with tarot archetypes so they become your guides to the inner realms. I recommend the Rider-Waite Tarot deck for beginners because it is the most popular tarot deck and is readily available. It is the model for many modern tarot decks and is easy to use. If you are an advanced tarot practitioner it's okay to use another deck that you know.

Lastly, suggestions of appropriate flower essence remedies for specific problems are listed in each chapter. Flower essences are dilute extracts of various types of flowers and plants that are similar to homeopathic remedies. Dr. Edward Bach, a famous English physician, developed the first remedies in the 1930s. Bach believed that diseases are a result of conflicts between body, mind, and spirit. The flower remedies act to balance these imbalances in the emotional and spiritual body, and bring about a gentle healing by treating the soul issue.

Invitation to Change

In *Karmic Healing* you will enter a new world. I will teach you how to access your spirit, develop your inner awareness, and claim your psychic power. You will discover where your karmic blocks are and how to release them.

You don't have to believe in reincarnation to gain something of value from this book. Just as you can practice yoga without becoming a Hindu, you can accept past lives as a philosophy without subscribing to a religious doctrine.

You will have a unique experience. As you work with your journal, you'll create a magical place of secrets, a safe space for your thoughts and feelings, and a haven for you to reveal yourself to yourself. Welcome to the most exciting voyage of this life or any other—your karmic healing journey!

Part I

karmic healing tools

your inner world

Any time you explore the unknown, it is good to have a guide so you'll know what to expect. When you go deep within yourself, you are literally delving into another world. In this chapter, I'll guide you through techniques to navigate this new territory. You'll learn how to focus your mind and relax your body, the keys to opening up your psychic senses. As you develop your psychic muscles, you'll also learn how to access wisdom from your higher self. You'll be introduced to the healing power of flower essences. Learning these techniques will prepare you for many wonderful experiences as you embark on your karmic journey.

How Your Past Enters Your Present

When Heather was eighteen, she was diagnosed as having an ovarian cyst, which was the size of a grapefruit. After having surgery to remove the cyst, she developed endometriosis and suffered from severe menstrual cramps. A few years later, her cyst grew back so she had surgery again. The doctors predicted the cyst would be a lifelong problem and prescribed birth control pills as a remedy.

No matter how low the dosage, the hormones made Heather feel like she was on an emotional roller coaster. One minute she was laughing, the next she'd be raging with anger. She began suffering from headaches, and she retained so much water that she felt like a bloated whale. Moreover, she no longer enjoyed sex with her beloved husband because it was too painful. It put a strain on her marriage.

Heather felt trapped in a vicious cycle. If she took the other medications the doctors prescribed, she'd either go right to sleep or be so lethargic that she felt like a zombie. She couldn't drive a car if she took those pills. If she couldn't drive, she couldn't go to work. She suffered with this chronic condition for twelve years, switching physicians occasionally in the search for new advice.

Heather thought she was doomed to endure her condition forever. However, one night when she rented a movie a strange thing happened. As she watched the rape scene in the film *The Accused,* she became physically sick to her stomach and so upset that she couldn't sit through to the ending. She thought her reaction was odd, since she never had been molested or attacked.

The next day, while standing in line at a health food store, Heather happened to pick up my brochure. As she read my description of the past-life regression process, she became intrigued; perhaps a past-life experience could explain her intense emotional reaction to the movie. However, she was afraid that her husband wouldn't approve. He'd probably think she had lost her mind. She scheduled an appointment despite her fears.

Before the regression, I asked Heather to temporarily put aside her skepticism. I coached her to trust the images she would see in her mind's eye even if they were weird or strange.

During her regression, Heather reclined on a massage table while soft music played in the background. I began the hypnosis process by talking to her in a soothing tone of voice. She began to relax and go deep into a trance. She visualized taking a train ride back through time and space into another lifetime. When the train stopped and the door opened, this was what she experienced:

"I am a pretty fifteen-year-old girl, holding a basket in my hand. My name is Rosita. It's light and sunny. I'm in South America somewhere. I'm a little scared. I'm at an outdoor market. There are many vendors selling vegetables, animals, clothes. . . . I am bringing a piece of cloth to sell to one of the vendors. Men at the market stare at me. I don't like the way they look at me. I want to go home."

I asked Heather to move to the source of her problem.

"I live with my parents and my sister. My father hits my mother. She doesn't stand up to him at all. Around the house, we are just treated like servants."

Heather began to sob.

"I'm leaving. I'm moving out of the house. A man comes to marry me. Or he bought me? It's the same for me as with my mother. Marriage is an economic arrangement. I'm scared. We are walking, carrying big bags. This man is in his fifties, yet I am only a teenager."

Heather was silent for a few minutes and cried again.

"Oh my God! He rapes me! He uses me to satisfy himself. It's disgusting. He is vulgar and ugly."

When Heather stopped crying, I asked her to give her pain an image. She imagined her remaining grief as a thorny shrub growing in her uterus. She visualized cutting it down with large garden shears. When the shrub disappeared, she visualized filling the empty space with the golden light of healing energy.

I asked her to scan that life and be open to any other information she may receive.

"All of the women in the whole village had no respect. They were treated like second-class citizens."

Heather visualized Rosita in a pink bubble of light. She sent her love and acceptance to Rosita and released her into the white light of universal love. Heather gave every cell of her body permission to function in perfect health and perfect vitality. We then affirmed that Heather is a beautiful woman who deserves to be sexually satisfied.

When Heather came out of trance, she felt peaceful and lighter. I suggested that she take the flower essence of crab apple—to continue releasing feelings of shame that may have accumulated from that lifetime—mixed with alpine lily, to integrate her sexuality with her feminine self.

The next day, Heather got her period for the first time in two years. Her cycle has been regular ever since. One year later, her gynecologist gave her a clean bill of health. There were no signs of cysts or endometriosis. Her menstrual cramps used to be so horrible that she was bedridden. Since our regression session, her painful cramps have disappeared. She hasn't had to take hormones, and she feels really good. A few years later, she sent me a Christmas card with a photo of her two children.

Karmic Clog

There is no proof that Heather lived in South America in another time. That doesn't matter. What's important is that the karmic healing process gave her a context to connect with her unresolved soul issue and transform it.

Watching the rape scene in a movie triggered Heather's unresolved feelings of being sexually abused. After twelve years of gynecological problems, she was finally ready to deal with the emotional component of her wounded sexuality. We'll never know whether she was *really* raped in a past life. Maybe deep down she felt that having a competitive job in the business world "raped" her femininity.

Heather's regression helped her restore her self-worth as a woman and reinvent her sex life. Although she had received medical treatment for her physical symptoms, she had not treated her soul issue and thus had not healed.

As we now know, the body, mind, and spirit relate together holistically. Unresolved soul issues can create energetic blockages that I call "karmic clogs." These blockages affect the way we think, feel, behave, and experience our body. Heather's unresolved soul issue had impacted her emotional and physical well-being.

What's unresolved from your past can be carried over into your present. In Heather's case, cysts and endometriosis were symptoms of a deeper problem. She felt powerless as a woman. Once the block containing Heather's trauma was released during her regression, she was free of the *karmic clog* that had affected her health. She felt better, and her marriage improved. She was no longer restricted by mood swings and physical pain. Heather gained the inner freedom to create a richer life. This is what karmic healing is all about.

Five Techniques for Karmic Healing

Using Heather's experience as a model, let's examine how you can explore past lives on your own. These are the techniques you'll have to master to have healing and transformation take place:

- **Set an intention:** Decide what you want to change. Knowing what you want is the first step in having what you want.

- **Relax:** Calm your mind and body. This will help you open the doors of communication to your higher self.
- **Be receptive:** Use your psychic senses to access the wisdom of your soul.
- **Visualize well-being:** Resolve issues by combining visual symbols and affirmations.
- **Treat with flower essences:** Take flower essences to help keep you on track and avoid relapsing into old patterns.

Heather was not aware that her gynecological problems were related to a past life. She came into my office with a desire to know why she had overreacted when watching a movie. Out of her *intention* to learn about herself, she discovered the root cause of her suffering. Resolving her health problem came as a total surprise to her.

By deeply *relaxing*, Heather was able to receive information from her higher self. By being *receptive* to her higher self, she received the message that it was time for her to deal with the emotional component of her health issues. Even though she's beautiful and physically fit, she did not feel comfortable with her femininity. She was unaware that she felt powerless as a woman.

When Heather assigned a visual symbol to represent her grief, she was able to release the trauma trapped in her body's cell memory. She *visualized* cutting down a thorny shrub and filling her pelvis with light to release the blockage. She then reprogrammed her mind by affirming her femininity and power. The final step was to take a flower essence for one month following her regression to keep the transformational process moving forward. The flower essence acted as a *treatment* and helped her to integrate the changes into her life.

Accessing your inner world is simple, once you know how. Like learning any skill, the more you practice, the better you become. Your efforts will be rewarded. You may feel awkward when you begin practicing these techniques. But the more you work with them, the easier they will become.

Set an Intention

Knowing what you want is the first step toward making it happen. That's why it's important to set goals. What do you want to accomplish by exploring your karma and your past lives?

On the top of the first page of your journal, write the question: "What do I want?"

Now answer the question. Define your goals. Be specific. For example, your responses may be something like the following:

- I want to know the source of my weight problem.
- I want to know why my relationship with my mother is so difficult.
- I want to know why I have to struggle to make ends meet.
- I want to know why I am afraid of water.
- I want to know why I love French culture.
- I want to learn whether I know my husband from another life.

Take your time writing your intentions. You can set as many goals as you'd like. The clearer you are about what you want, the better results you will have.

Now set a time line. Be realistic about the amount of time you can commit to doing the exercises and meditations. Do you want to finish a chapter per week or per month?

Are you going to practice the exercises in the morning, after dinner, or before bedtime?

Schedule the time in your appointment book or personal organizer. You may even want to set an alarm using your computer or establish other reminders.

Next, build a support team. You may want to share what you are doing with a friend or two so they can support your efforts. Who can coach you through the changes you'll be making? Who will help keep you on track if the going gets rough? Schedule some coaching calls or emails.

Finally, write a letter to yourself stating what you want to accomplish. What do you have at stake? Why is it important to do this work? How can you benefit from karmic healing?

When you finish your letter, make three photocopies. Place them in self-addressed stamped envelopes. Note on your schedule to mail them to yourself when you are beginning chapters 3, 5, and 7 of this book. At those times you'll want to remind yourself that this is important, counteracting any resistance to progressing. It's natural to resist change because it is easier and more comfortable to coast along. Achieving anything worthwhile takes perseverance, commitment, and determination. Any desired result, from losing weight to winning a gold medal, requires exerting some effort. If you want to succeed, you have to train yourself to go outside your comfort zone. You have to persist when you confront the barriers that are blocking you from actualizing your intention. The power of sticking to your commitment to yourself will allow you to triumph.

Relax

Relaxation is the key to accessing your psychic senses. Being able to relax your body at will is used as a self-hypnosis technique and as a yoga practice. When you can focus your mind on one thing, you begin to harness the power of concentration. It is the key to training your mind and body to harmonize.

Creating a sacred space in your home will support you in transcending the ordinary world into the spiritual realm. It's good to set up a room or a place in a room to practice the exercises in this book. You'll want to find a quiet place where you won't be disturbed. When you're there, shut off your cell phone, place your pager on vibrate, and allow voice mail to answer your incoming calls. Let family members know you're taking some time for yourself and you won't be available. Use a couch or clear a space on the floor to lie down. It's nice to use a mat, futon, or towel as a cushion if you're on the floor.

You might set up a music system so you can play meditative music.

Once you've found a good location, you can create an altar by using a small table, a mantel, or a scarf on the floor. Find a picture of your favorite god or goddess, angel, spiritual teacher, power animal, ancestor, or saint to place in the center of your altar. You can include a religious symbol that has meaning for you, like a cross, pentacle, or Star of David. You can also add a natural object, such as a crystal, rock, semiprecious stone, seashell, or feather. It's nice to include candles and incense.

Creating a sacred space will also suggest to your subconscious that you're taking your spiritual explorations seriously. Just as a comfortable bedroom promotes restful sleep, using one special place for your past-life studies will help you build a reservoir of psychic energy, allowing you to relax into trance states. After a few weeks of constant use, you'll feel a peaceful atmosphere in your sacred space.

What to Expect While in Trance

When you enter a deep state of relaxation, you may feel very heavy, as if your body has melted into the floor. Or you may sense your body as very light, floating up by the ceiling. It's possible to become very hot. Feeling intense heat is a good sign. It means you're accessing healing energy. You may be aware of tingling sensations, or ripples of electricity pulsating throughout your being. Some people see colors in their mind's eye; others feel as though they're flooded with light. You may feel like you're spinning. All of these experiences are common. There's no one "right" way.

While doing a deep relaxation exercise, you may become aware of tension or pain that you've been holding in your body, just as you may feel soreness in your muscles if you've just returned from the gym. Allow yourself to be aware of the soreness. Experiencing the discomfort will often release the pain.

If you've been suppressing an emotion, it probably will surface so you become aware of it. Some people experience sadness or even anger when they go into trance. While relaxed, if you experience an emotion, allow yourself to feel it and then let it go. Experiencing the feeling will release it.

Some people can't relax and are uncomfortable with their racing minds. If you find that happening to you, be patient. Relaxing deeply will require some practice. You may want to lower your intake of caffeine and sugar. I recommend taking a yoga or a tai chi class or doing deep breathing. Engage in any activity that helps you focus. These practices allow you to master your mind and travel to altered states of consciousness with greater ease.

Relaxation Exercise

Before you begin practicing the following relaxation technique, make sure you'll be really comfortable. It's good to support your lower back by placing a pillow underneath your knees while lying on your back. Make sure you'll be warm enough. Your body temperature lowers when you go into trance, and there's a tendency to get cold. Cover yourself with a wrap or blanket.

Allow yourself ten minutes to complete this exercise. You may want to record it on tape, pausing one minute between each instruction. Do the following:

- Lay on your back, with your arms at your sides and your palms facing up.
- Feel the relaxing power entering the toes of your feet. Feel it moving down into your arches, down through your heels, and through the soles of your feet.
- The relaxing power moves into your calves and up into your knees.
- Allow your thighs to totally relax.
- Release your pelvis, hips, and lower back.
- Relax your torso and rib cage.
- Relax all the muscles in your shoulders and neck.
- Release your arms and hands. Let your palms and fingers go limp.
- Relax all the muscles in your face.
- Relax all the muscles in your eyes.
- Your total body is relaxed.
- Savor the pleasant sensation of total relaxation.

Practice this at least once a day, and your life will change. You'll be able to release stress and strain with ease and feel more peace and contentment. Keep track of your progress by making notes in your journal. You'll see an improvement in no time at all.

Be Receptive

You experience the physical world through your five senses: taste, touch, sight, smell, and hearing. Through these faculties, you interact with your outer environment. You can tell whether something looks good, tastes bad, or sounds pleasant. However, each sense has a range of subtleties. The quality of your experience corresponds to your sensitivity to these subtleties. To enhance your sensitivity, you can fine-tune your physical senses.

Wine connoisseurs perfect their palates. In one sip, they can detect a hint of spice, the flavor of chocolate, or the subtle taste of mint. People with uneducated taste buds, on the other hand, can't tell the difference between a Beaujolais and a Cabernet.

Artists cultivate a trained eye, and they can distinguish subtleties of color and style. Upon looking at a portrait, for example, they can tell whether a skin tone color is warm or cool. People with an untrained eye will only see the color field of flesh.

Musicians develop an acute ear. They know whether you're singing out of tune, in the wrong key, or off tempo. Someone with an unrefined ear, however, will only sense that something sounds odd.

Perfumers educate their nose, and they know whether an aroma is a blend of jasmine and rose, or neroli and sandalwood. The average person may not be able to distinguish between the perfume of a real rose and an artificial scent.

Massage therapists develop a perceptive touch. Their sensitive fingers can discern the knots in your shoulders, and then can untie them. Without such training, most people couldn't feel the difference between a shirt made of polyester and another made of silk.

Get my point? Developing your senses brings quality to the way you experience life. There's nothing wrong with not being able to differentiate polyester from silk. Preferring fast food to gourmet fare doesn't make you a bad person. However, there's an extra richness that is only available when your senses are refined and attuned to sensory subtleties.

One of your senses may be more developed than the others. Your taste buds may be sensitive though you are lacking in tactile refinement. You may have a trained ear but have no visual acumen. Or vice versa. The same is true with your *psychic senses*.

As you experience your *outer* world through your physical senses, so you experience your *inner* world through your *psychic senses*. You recall your past lives and receive information from your higher self mostly through the following faculties:

- Clairvoyance, which means *clear seeing*
- Claircognizance, which means *clear knowing*
- Clairsentience, which means *clear feeling*

As with our physical senses, we have all developed our psychic senses to different degrees. In my workshops, before doing a past-life regression, I ask participants to visualize their kitchens. This provides them an opportunity to use their psychic senses and determine how developed they may be.

Since most people are visually oriented, most people have stronger clairvoyant abilities. They can close their eyes and recall a clear image of their kitchen. They can see it in their mind's eye in perfect detail and in color, as if they were looking at a photograph. When these people receive a message while in trance, it will come to them as an image of some sort.

But some people just can't visualize such scenes. For instance, when they try to picture their kitchen in their mind, all they see is black. Those with claircognizant ability may receive data from their higher selves in the form of a sense of knowing something, in this case, their kitchen. When you know who is calling you as the phone rings (and you don't have caller ID) you are using this psychic sense.

Other people are clairsentient; they trust their hunches or their gut feelings. In their day-to-day life, these people are empathetic and can usually intuit what other people are thinking or feeling. They get a sense of their kitchen when they try to picture it, rather than visualizing it. They may not be able to envision a past-life memory; instead they may just get a feeling in their body.

Other psychic senses that are less commonly developed include clairgustance, or clear tasting, the ability to taste a substance without putting anything in the mouth; clairaudience, or clear hearing, the ability to receive spiritual messages through songs or sounds; clairolfactory, or clear smelling, the ability to smell a fragrance coming from the spiritual realms; and clairtangency, or clear touching, also called psychometry, the skill of holding an object and gathering previously unknown information about the article, its owner, or its history.

On rare occasions people have had psychic olfactory experiences during a past-life regression. I have only known two clients who have experienced a past-life memory through clairgustance. One recalled being an Inuit Indian or Eskimo, and she had a taste of fish in her mouth during the regression. The other client recalled being an amputee begging on the streets of Hong Kong, and he tasted what he believed to be opium.

You Are Unique

Everyone experiences a past life differently. Our psychic senses are developed at various levels, so we retrieve information from our inner selves using different psychic senses.

Marty, whom I regressed at a New Age conference, provides an example of different levels of psychic senses at work during regression. Marty was soft-spoken and shy. Every time he tried to share his beliefs and ideas, he'd have an anxiety attack. His heart would race and his palms would sweat.

When he went into a deep state of relaxation, Marty traveled back in time to thousands of years ago. While in trance, he *saw* himself as a man wearing a long white robe standing in an open-air market in the center of a small town somewhere in the Middle East (clairvoyance). He also *knew* he was a preacher and that he traveled from town to town (claircognizance).

When I asked him to move to the source of his problem, he said, "I see that I'm surrounded by a mob of angry people."

He then had an *emotional* reaction—fear—and started to breathe rapidly. He said in terror, "They are throwing stones at me!"

When I asked him what happened, he said, "I have a pain in my rib cage. It's as though my chest has been crushed." Marty *felt* that the right side of his ribcage was being crushed (clairsentience). He didn't see it.

I asked Marty to release the memory of this traumatic death by visualizing a large stone being lifted from his chest. As the stone rolled away, he exhaled a deep sigh of relief.

Marty didn't receive a long drawn-out story in his past-life regression. He didn't know his name, the exact year, or a specific place. Rather, he received a few impressions, which led to a breakthrough in his ability to express himself.

Marty experienced an immediate transformation. During the rest of the conference, many people commented that he seemed a changed man. In the classrooms he often had his hand up, wanting to share. When he was called on, he was able to speak freely, with ease.

Fine-Tuning Your Psychic Senses

Just as you can refine your physical senses, you can also sharpen your inner faculties, your psychic senses. You can learn to tone these muscles; work those psychic muscles! Remember, though, if you're out of shape, you don't begin by lifting heavy weights; you'll probably strain yourself, get frustrated, and defeat your purpose. You begin by lifting lighter weights until you feel comfortable, strong, and flexible. Then you go on to heavier weights. Honing psychic skills takes practice and requires patience.

Crystals can enhance access to your soul wisdom. A single terminated quartz crystal placed on your forehead pointing down can amplify your ability to visualize. Holding a crystal in your hand as you practice the meditations can also intensify your experience.

Psychic-Enhancing Flower Essences, Plants, and Crystals
Try working with one or more of the following elements to support your healing process:

- **Mugwort:** enhances your psychic ability (sleeping with a dream pillow made of dried mugwort leaves can improve your ability to remember your dreams)
- **White chestnut flower essence:** helps quiet your mind
- **Impatiens flower essence:** overcomes resistance to committing time to cultivate your inner life
- **Moonstone crystal:** aids your psychic receptivity when you wear it
- **Quartz crystal:** when placed underneath your pillow, helps your subconscious mind resolve problems while you sleep

Discover Your Psychic Senses Exercise
The first step in experiencing a past life is to uncover which of your psychic senses is strongest; this will usually correspond to the way you generally receive information. Are you more visual, cognizant, or feeling oriented? Use your journal to document your experience.

You may want to record this simple exercise on tape, so you can practice it and master this technique. If so, give yourself three minutes to complete the visualization. Speak slowly and softly, pausing briefly after each sentence.

Arrange not to be disturbed. Leave all your worries behind. Go to the sacred space you have created. If it's night, turn down the lights. If it's daytime, pull down the shades. Light a candle or burn some incense to create a peaceful atmosphere. Play some soft music to set a quiet mood.

Stretch out in a comfortable position in your sacred space. Close your eyes and take a deep breath. Practice the body relaxation technique. Feel your breath move through your body like a gentle wave. When you inhale, inhale peace. On your exhale, let go of any tension. Inhale, breathe in relaxation. Exhale, let go a little more. Continue breathing deeply for a minute or two.

With your eyes closed, recall your present kitchen. Look down at the floor. Of what material is it made? How does it feel against your bare feet? What's the temperature in the room? How does the air feel against your skin? What color are the walls? Do you hear any sounds? Do you notice any smells? Notice the sink. Are there dishes in it? Or is it empty? Go over and touch something that attracts your attention. What does it feel like?

Now just let all this go. Get a sense of the room you're actually in. Feel your body. Slowly open your eyes, and return to the present.

Record your experience by answering the following questions in your journal. How was your clairvoyant experience?

- Was your kitchen a picture? If so sketch it, even if you think you can't draw. Could you see it in detail?
- Could you see if there were dishes in the sink or was it empty?
- Did you notice any colors?
- Did you feel as though you were watching a movie of your kitchen?

How was your clairsentient experience?

- Could you feel the air against your skin or the floor against your bare feet?
- What object attracted your attention? Did you touch it? What did it feel like?

- Write down any body sensations you experienced.
- Did you feel as though you were standing in your kitchen?
- Did you notice any sounds or smells?

How was your claircognizant experience?

- Were you unable to see or feel anything in your kitchen but just *knew* the color of the walls, the temperature of the room, and whether there were dishes in the sink?
- Were you unable to see or feel a special object but knew what that object was?
- Did you feel as though you were floating in your kitchen?

How was your overall experience?

- Did you go to a kitchen that wasn't familiar?
- Did you visit more than one kitchen?
- Write down any emotions you felt while recalling your kitchen.
- Did you recall a childhood memory? If so, is your higher self telling you to release something?
- Are you more visual, cognizant, or feeling oriented?

Most people have a combination of visual, knowing, and feeling perceptions. Whatever you experience is right for you. No way is better than any other.

Sometimes people begin to process memories from their childhood after doing this simple exercise. While leading a group session, I asked all the participants to share their experiences. One man had recalled the kitchen of his childhood. His family had been very poor, and tears welled up in his eyes as he released a painful memory. One woman with a weight problem discovered being in her kitchen was not pleasant; anger and anxiety surfaced during the exercise, and she realized that every time she was upset, she raided the refrigerator. Some people go to kitchens from other lifetimes. One woman recalled a kitchen in a log cabin without indoor plumbing, not a kitchen she had ever known in this lifetime.

Practice recalling your kitchen to become more comfortable with flexing your psychic muscles. This exercise will prepare you to retrieve information while in trance and to visualize releasing your problems. Trust your experience as you learn to navigate your inner world.

Clairsentience Exercise

Though many people find that their strongest psychic sense is clairvoyance, if you found that your *feeling* psychic sense is strongest, you have clairsentient abilities. Your gut feelings have a strong kinesthetic component. You may have a physical sensation somewhere in your body or have an emotional response when this psychic sense is in operation. Although called gut feelings, your intuition may not be located in your stomach. Your clairsentience may be felt in another part of your body. To find out what part of your body is most receptive to psychic stimuli, try this exercise.

- Recall a time when you had a clairsentient experience. Perhaps it was a first impression when you met someone new. Maybe you had a good feeling when you were introduced, and the person later proved to be a supportive friend.
- Remember yourself in that moment. How did you look? How did you sound? What physical sensations did you have in your body? What emotions did you feel?

The more specific you can be in describing the physical signs that accompanied your clairsentient experience, the easier it will be for you to acknowledge and trust this ability in the future.

Visualize Well-Being

Now that you've set your intention, learned to relax, and discovered how to be receptive while in trance, the next step is to learn to be actively creative with your mind by using visualization.

Visualization will enable you to release karmic clogs or energy blocks connected to your soul issue. These blocks are composed of buried negative thoughts and emotions related to past experiences.

When we don't transform our grief, rage, hatred, or fear into love and forgiveness, we suppress energy that should be released. It then becomes stuck in our energy field. When we don't heal our pain, our suppressed thoughts and judgments crystallize into self-sabotaging attitudes and automatic responses. Blocks often include body sensations such as tension, tightness, or pain.

For example, suppose you find your lover is cheating on you. Instead of resolving the issue, you never speak to him or her again. By being unforgiving, you hold onto anger. You make a decision to never love again. Ten years later, you may be single, lonely, and wanting a partner. Somehow, you've gained twenty pounds that has settled around your midriff, creating a protective barrier. Over the years, you've developed digestive problems. You wonder why you can't seem to attract a partner, even though you socialize and have employed a dating service. You can't seem to meet anyone special because you have forgotten you've made a decision not to love. This thought-form lies embedded in the pain of betrayal deep within your being, along with the fear of being vulnerable to another person. Unknowingly, you've buried the rage, fear, and grief in your midriff.

Blocks can be big or small, depending on the size of the problem. Issues dealing with trauma or abuse are going to take longer to heal. Often these clogs accumulate lifetime after lifetime, until we are ready to deal with the issues and release them.

Every healing session you do will be different. Sometimes your session will be light and exhilarating. Others may seem heavy and profound.

The key to visualization is to focus your mind, which will improve your ability to concentrate. This technique will help you in every aspect of your life. You'll be able to perform simple tasks more quickly, directing your attention to one thing at a time without being distracted. The following four visualization exercises should take more than five minutes each.

Afterimage Visualization

Sit up straight in a comfortable chair in a darkened room. Place a lit candle about two feet in front of you at eye level. Stare into the candle flame for a few minutes. When you close your eyes, you'll still be able to see the flame in your mind's eye. Focus on this afterimage for a minute or two. Practice this until you can sustain the image of the candle flame in your mind's eye for five minutes. Track your progress in your journal.

Tarot Card Visualization

Purchase a pack of Rider-Waite tarot cards. Take out the card labeled The Magician. Sit upright in a chair, with your spine straight, and place the card on a table in front of you. Focus on the card. Take in the whole image—the colors, the figure, the roses and lilies in the garden, and the table. Close your eyes and see how much of the card you can recall in your mind's eye. Practice this until you can recall the card in detail.

Once you've mastered the art of creatively visualizing, it's important to learn how to dissolve your images. Practice the following exercise until you can perform it with ease.

Image-Destroying Visualization

Sit upright in a chair with your spine straight. Imagine a white rose enclosed in a pink bubble of light floating about a foot in front of you. Once you've imagined it, imagine it disappearing. Practice creating and destroying this image each day for about five minutes until you can do it easily.

When you can creatively visualize and dematerialize images, you will be able to reprogram your consciousness. This technique will allow you to release negative patterns and imprint new positive images.

Karmic Healing Visualization

Now that you are able to visualize creating and dissolving images, you are ready to experience the formula that will allow you to dissolve a karmic clog or energy block.

1. While in a state of deep relaxation, scan your entire body.
2. Acknowledge any tightness, pain, or heaviness.
3. Assign an image to the body sensation. Does it feel like a lead ball in your chest? A wad of chewing gum in your throat? An erupting volcano in your stomach? Give it a specific image.
4. What color is it? How much does it weigh? What kind of material is it made of?
5. Once you've ascribed a color, shape, weight, and substance to your body sensation, you are ready to destroy the image.

Decide how you want to get rid of the image you created. Be creative. You can visualize Martians taking it up into outer space, or blowing it up with explosives. You can visualize your favorite cartoon character eating it up. *It's very important that you destroy your image of your energy block*.

Once the visualized image you've created is gone, you must replace it with white light. Fill that space in your body with the light of universal love. Sometimes I use specific colors, but that's a more advanced technique. Working with basic white light will work fine.

When you've completed visualizing the light, it's time to use an affirmation. Affirmations are positive thoughts you repeatedly suggest to your subconscious. They can help you achieve your goals by changing your attitude, replacing negative thoughts with positive ones. You can change any thought into an affirmation. For instance, "I'm not good enough" can be changed to "I'm perfect just the way that I am." At the end of each meditation, you will be guided to use this technique to heal and transform. I'll include some suggestions for affirmation at the end of each meditation, but feel free to wing it and make up your own.

Treat with Flower Essences

The final step in the karmic healing process is to take a flower essence for a month to reinforce your healing session. It's not absolutely necessary, but I've found that this enhances your ability to transform.

Flowers have always been used to express our emotions. We use them at weddings, celebrations, and holidays to express our joy. Sending flowers on Valentine's Day declares a message of love, and a hand-delivered bouquet renders an apology. A vase of flowers next to a person in a hospital bed conveys a wish for recovery. A spray sent to a funeral supports us in our grief and mourning.

Dr. Edward Bach, a British physician and scientist, discovered that specific flowers can help certain emotional and mental conditions. The flowers' subtle energy provides their healing potency. Commercial flower essences contain infinitesimal amounts of the plant material. Flowers are picked at the peak of their blossoming period and put into glass containers with distilled water for about three hours while exposed to sunlight. The flowers are then discarded, and the remaining water is preserved in brandy. The water's molecular structure is charged and imprinted with the soul pattern of the flowers' vibrational essence. It is this plant signature that heals.

Flower essences can enhance one's inner experiences, help release emotional trauma and self-defeating thought patterns, and clear up other problems, such as indecision, fear, mental exhaustion, or hopelessness. They are nontoxic and nonaddictive, and can be used safely with other medications. It's better to take very small amounts of a flower essence over a longer period of time than to take them all at once. Two drops, four times a day is an average dosage. Essences are taken under the tongue, in a glass of water, or rubbed behind your earlobes.

Flower essences have become so popular that many other companies, besides Bach Flowers, have sprung up over the years. Suggested flower remedies for you to choose from accompany each chapter of the book, and a list of resources appears in the appendix.

Summary

Now that you have learned the basic techniques of karmic healing—set an intention, relax, be receptive, visualize well-being, and treat with flower essences—you can begin to explore how karma operates in your life. If you're new to this work, be patient with yourself. Once you master the relaxation, concentration, and visualization exercises, your life will improve whether you ever experience a past life or not. Practice does make perfect. If you take the time to do the work, your efforts will be rewarded. In the next chapter you will learn how to uncover your karmic blocks, detect your unresolved soul issues, and begin to heal.

Chapter Two

Random Acts of Healing

You don't have to believe in past lives to benefit from the karmic healing process. When you are ready to heal at your core, you attract specific circumstances that trigger intense emotions, which arise unexpectedly. These feelings, connected to unresolved soul issues, may not be solely related to present circumstances. In this chapter, you will learn how to detect, trigger, and resolve your issues by applying the four karmic healing steps: retrieve, remember, reprogram, and reinforce.

Karmic Pop-Ups

Have you ever experienced déjà vu? You walk into a café and you feel as though you've been there before, but it's your first visit there. You watch a documentary about the French Revolution and it seems very familiar, even though you didn't really study it in detail in school. You visit a foreign country and it's as though you've returned home. There's no way you can explain these feelings that seem unrelated to the present.

I call irrational emotions and responses that seem to surface out of context *karmic pop-ups* because they pop up unpredictably. They are your soul's way of getting you to pay attention.

Karmic pop-ups are a kind of wake-up call. They can rise to our conscious awareness when we least expect them. Most of the time, we're not aware of the source of these inexplicable feelings. Sometimes our reactions are so overwhelming we are motivated to seek professional help, as in the case of Jamilla. Although she had a past-life experience long before she met me, she was eager to share her story because it was so powerful.

Jamilla was haunted by the same recurring dream for years.

"I am standing at the top of a stairwell in a dungeon. Two men dressed as guards are holding each of my arms. They are forcing me to walk down the stairs toward a huge wooden door. My heart pounds as I try to cry out, but no sound comes when I open my mouth. As I reach the door, I awaken. Beads of perspiration pour down my forehead, and my throat is parched."

Jamilla never thought her dream had anything to do with a past life, just as she never thought her fear of entering crowded elevators was significant. However, she changed her mind when she traveled to Africa on a pilgrimage to connect with her roots. During her stay in Ghana she had a wonderful time, enjoying the people, the countryside, and the seaside. But when she visited the slave castles on the Gold Coast, she became nervous and anxious.

In the late fifteenth century, captive villagers were imprisoned in these "castles" before they were put on ships and sold as slaves. The castles were places of torture, suffering, and pain. When the tour guide invited Jamilla to descend the stairs to see "the door of no return," she experienced a karmic pop-up.

Jamilla's heart began to race, and she became fearful that something terrible was going to happen. She was so upset that she couldn't continue with the rest of the tour. She left the castle and waited in the tour bus for her husband and the rest of her group. She didn't feel like herself until she got on the plane to return home on the following day.

She was so shaken by her experience at the slave castles that she sought a past-life regression when she returned to the United States. In a trance state, Jamilla immediately went to the staircase of her recurring nightmares; it was the staircase in the slave castle that led to the dungeon.

"Oh my God! There are people shackled to the wall. Some are being branded with hot irons! The stench is unbearable."

While deep in trance, Jamilla gasped for air. She started coughing as if she were choking. She cried out in terror.

"It's so quiet. I can't bear the silence. They're all dead. I'm the only one left."

Her chest heaved as she released the deep-seated grief she had held in her heart. She reported later that she needed a good night's sleep after her session, but at last she slept peacefully.

It's been eight years since the regression, and Jamilla has never had that nightmare again. Her fear of being in crowded elevators also disappeared. She reported that since the regression, she discovered that her historic colonial home was part of the Underground Railroad. It was an odd coincidence that abolitionists used her basement to hide slaves escaping north to freedom before the Civil War.

The Four Steps to Karmic Healing

Now you're ready to practice karmic healing by following these easy steps:

- **Retrieve:** Pinpoint your karmic issues by answering specific questions in the emotional, physical, and mental karmic detectors segments. Then ask your higher self for guidance as you practice the following triggering exercises.
- **Remember:** Recall your past-life data by practicing regression meditation.

- **Reprogram:** Use visualizations and affirmations to release negative patterns and imprint new positive images into your mind.
- **Reinforce:** Take particular flower essences to reinforce your new attitudes and behaviors.

Pick a goal from your journal. What do you want to explore? The clearer you are about your intention to heal, the easier it will be to know when you've been triggered.

Triggering exercises fall into three categories: emotional, physical, and mental. You may find that one category is better suited for you. If so, keep working with that category until you are triggered. When you are triggered, you'll then proceed to the Magic Mirror Meditation (later in this chapter). Begin the karmic healing process by answering the questions in the following exercise.

Karmic Triggers—Retrieve

If you can accept that we are here on earth to learn and develop our spirituality, life becomes a sacred gift. Every experience can bring us closer to our own enlightenment. Experiencing karmic pop-ups is a blessing. Even if our emotional reactions seem unpleasant or difficult, they provide an opportunity to transform. If we take action, when our inner self prompts us to do spiritual development work, we can break free from karma's chains.

I call the circumstances that set off karmic pop-ups *karmic triggers*. When Jamilla visited the slave castles, it triggered her karmic pop-up. By seeking out a past-life therapist, she was able to release her recurring nightmare and heal her claustrophobia.

I don't recommend that you visit places where atrocities have been committed, unless you are prepared to deal with the trauma or unpleasant feelings that may be triggered. If you're suffering from severe anxiety or fear, please seek out a therapist to support you in healing.

What I do find, however, is that when you consciously ask your higher self for guidance, your requests are granted. But the message you receive may come about in a startling way. Karmic triggers fall into three categories: body, mind, and spirit. They can affect you emotionally, physically, or mentally.

Emotional Karmic Triggers

Visiting foreign countries, sacred sites, or even just a historic place can sometimes stimulate past-life material and affect you emotionally.

For instance, Marsha had an odd reaction while visiting a friend in Philadelphia. When she arrived at the door of the Victorian home her friend had just purchased, Marsha had an anxiety attack. Her heart pounded, and she broke out in a cold sweat. As she entered the house, something strange happened. The minute she walked through the door, she knew exactly where a fireplace had been bricked over and that a wall in the parlor had been removed. She knew the layout of the house before her friend gave her a tour of all the rooms. Every room she walked into felt familiar. But she couldn't bear to go into the bathroom. She couldn't tell her friend for fear that he would think she was crazy. So she just stood in the doorway and took a few deep breaths. As she stepped away, a warm wind blew her chill away and she felt safe and relieved.

Marsha was so unsettled by her experience that it affected her for weeks afterward. Finally, she overcame her initial apprehension to seek out spiritual guidance and called me. I suggested that a past-life regression might put her mind at ease. When she came to my office for her session, she was surprised by what she experienced during her regression.

"When I look down, I see a delicate white-skinned hand holding a silver-plated fork. I am sitting at a dinner table in a banquet hall. Larry, my husband's assistant, is seated to my left. My husband, Andrew, is on my right. He has dark hair, a well-trimmed beard, and big brown eyes. He cups my face with his hand and kisses me. I'm so very proud of him. The dinner is in his honor. He has just received some kind of an award.

"The master of ceremonies is asking me to stand. The whole room is applauding as I am acknowledged for my contribution to the project. My heart is going pitter-patter. As I sit down, I don't understand the glaring look that Larry gives to me."

Marsha knew that she's in Philadelphia and that her name was Deborah. When I asked her how she spent most of her time, she said, "I work for Andrew. I help him with his medical research."

I asked her to go to the source of her problem.

Marsha began to tremble and tears streamed down her face.

"I am relaxing in a big claw-footed bathtub. I hear the bathroom door creak open. Suddenly, a man comes up behind me and pushes my head under the water. I struggle to get up, but every time I do, my head is forced under the water again. I'm flailing my hands to fight off my attacker. I try to scream, but it's of no use. I am drowning. Before I lose consciousness, I see my murderer. It's Larry! He says, 'They should have been clapping for me.'"

Marsha continued to sob. When all of her sadness was released, she visualized pulling out a four-inch nail from her heart with a giant magnet. Marsha filled the empty feeling she had inside her heart with a rose-colored light, which brought her healing and peace.

When she came out of trance she said, "Wow! Did I really live here in Philadelphia in my friend's house? It explains why I've always had a fear of water. I've always preferred showers to baths and never learned to swim. I can't stand to be immersed in water. I get anxious just going to a pool."

I recommended that she take the flower essence mimulus to help her to continue to release her fear of water.

A month later Marsha phoned me from Atlantic City. It was the first time she had ever seen the Atlantic Ocean. She called to say, "I did it! I actually went into the water. It was fun! It was a bonus from doing the regression."

Marsha never expected that a visit to a friend's house would lead her on a healing journey to release her fear of water. You might think it was simply a coincidence that brought her to that house. But when coincidences or synchronicities happen, it's usually a message from our higher self telling us to pay attention.

Your Emotional Karmic Detectors

Here's the first step in the karmic healing process: *retrieve.* Ask yourself the following questions to detect karmic material related to your emotional experiences, then write down your responses:

- Do you prefer hot or cold weather? How do you feel when the weather is sticky and humid? Cold, damp, and foggy?
- Do you prefer to be in mountains? Rain forests? Deserts? Woods? Jungles? What's special about being in that type of land? How does being there nourish you?
- Do you prefer to be at the beach? At the ocean? At a lake? By a river? What's special about being by that type of water?
- Do you prefer to live in the city or the country? Why?
- Where do you like to go on vacation? Do you prefer to go to crowded, active cities or remote, wild places?
- Do you look for the hidden meaning when coincidences

occur in your life? Write a paragraph describing at least one important coincidence.

- What types of architecture do you love? Classical? Modern?
- Do you favor a particular style of house? Would it be made of adobe, stone, brick, logs, or something else? Do you prefer Victorian? Colonial? Ranch? Spanish style? Other? Are there particular styles of architecture that you dislike? Explain.
- Do you have a recurring dream? If so, write it down. Who are the main characters? What role do you play in the dream?
- Do you have phobias or irrational fears? What are they? When did the fear begin?
- What kind of music do you enjoy? Do you listen to international, classical, or folk music?

If the answers to these questions reveal an insight relating to your goal, continue working with the following exercise. If they don't seem to apply, begin reading the physical trigger section.

Your Emotional Karmic Triggers

Not all past-life memories are traumatic. Some karmic triggers bring pleasant feelings. You've probably noticed that music can affect your mood. Fast-paced music is energizing and makes you want to move your body. Slow music is relaxing.

Listening to music is a wonderful trigger for past-life pop-ups of an emotional nature. My student Mike was unexpectedly triggered while driving to work one morning, as he listened to Native American drumming on his car radio. Stopping at a red light, he had an extraordinary experience. The monotonous beat of the drum put him into a light trance and triggered a past-life memory to surface.

In his mind's eye, he saw a man with a bushy black beard. He knew that he was a trapper and that he lived in a Native American village in the 1700s. Feelings of love and acceptance warmed his heart, for he knew the tribe accepted him, even though he was a white man.

The feelings were so strong that his eyes welled up with tears. He was soon awakened from the trance by the sound of horns honking.

Emotional Karmic Triggers Exercise

To bring emotional past-life pop-ups into your conscious awareness, try one of these triggering techniques:

- Travel to unfamiliar towns, cities, or countries. Be aware of any unusual feelings that you have or coincidences that occur there.
- Listen to diverse kinds of music.
- Take a pilgrimage to a sacred power site. Many people have powerful experiences at places such as Stonehenge; the great Pyramids of Egypt; the Red Rocks of Sedona, Arizona; and the Serpent Mound in Ohio.
- Attend a live concert featuring the music of another culture or historical time period.
- Pay attention to the meaning of coincidences in your daily life.
- Be more in touch with your dreams by recording them in your journal each morning.

If you take on one of these suggestions and have an intense emotional reaction, or a gut feeling that you are experiencing a past life, you have been triggered. Do not continue to do the physical or mental trigger exercises. Move ahead to the Magic Mirror Meditation. If none of these triggering suggestions appeal to you, try answering the following physical triggering questions and suggestions.

Physical Karmic Triggers

Physical stimuli—such as attempting an unusual body posture, indulging in a beauty treatment, undergoing therapeutic body-work, or vigorous exercise—can stimulate a karmic pop-up.

Once I was triggered while having a foot paraffin treatment at a day spa. As the practitioner wrapped my waxed feet in plastic, my heart began to race. A thought flashed into my mind: "She is changing my bandages." In that moment, I knew I had lived in China and that I had had bound feet. The experience faded when the practitioner asked me if I was all right.

Later that day a friend told me that a local Chinese import store had some antique slippers of women who had had bound feet. I stopped by the shop to see them. The shopkeeper showed me the tiny beaded slippers. Reaching out to hold one, my hand began to tremble. I realized that I had four pairs of similar beaded slippers in my closet, handmade in China, all in my size. Odd coincidence?

I went home and looked up foot binding in Barbara Walker's *Women's Encyclopedia of Myths and Secrets.* It said: "The crippled woman was considered immeasurably charming by reason of her vulnerability and helplessness." These are issues that I've dealt with in this lifetime in some form or another.

Your Physical Karmic Detectors

To detect karmic pop-ups related to your physical experience, answer the following questions to *retrieve* information, then write down your responses:

- Make a list of your favorite foods. Are they different from what your mother cooked for you? What types of international cuisine do you enjoy? How do you feel while you are eating them?

- Make a list of the foods that you hate. Why do you dislike them? What countries are they from?

- Do you feel drawn to a particular sport or physical activity, such as mountain climbing, kayaking, tennis, hiking, sailing, or other? What do you love about them?

- Is it hard for you to express yourself through dance or other kinds of movement? Why is it a challenge?

- Do you enjoy collecting objects from a certain culture? Which culture? Do you enjoy collecting objects from a certain time period in history? What do you collect? Stamps? Guns? Teacups? Salt and pepper shakers? Fabrics? Clothes?

- Do you collect antiques? If so, from what period? From what country? What types of antiques fascinate you? Furniture? Cars? Costumes? Jewelry?

If the answers to these questions reveal an insight relating to your goal, continue working with the following exercise. If they don't seem to apply, begin reading the mental trigger section.

Your Physical Karmic Triggers

You may have had a past-life memory unexpectedly pop into your awareness but didn't know what it was. Now with practice, you are opening up the channels of communication with your higher self. As you consciously seek to know yourself, the information you retrieve will become clearer and clearer.

My client Jane had an unusual experience while getting a deep-tissue massage. When the massage therapist began to knead Jane's left thigh, she was triggered. An image of a big woman walking on a grassy hillside came into her mind's eye. She could see a stone cottage and smell the salty sea air. She knew that she was in Scotland in the early 1900s. The next moment she felt a sensation of coldness throughout her body. Her joints ached, and she knew that she had arthritis, though she didn't have the ailment in her present life. Moments later, the memory faded and the chill was replaced with a warm glow.

Physical Karmic Triggers Exercise
To bring physical past-life pop-ups into your conscious awareness, try one of these triggering techniques:

- Schedule a session of deep-tissue bodywork, acupuncture treatments, or rebirthing. Pay attention to any memories that surface.
- Do yoga postures that are more challenging than usual, especially inverted body poses.
- Go to a contact improvisational dance class. You can have a direct experience of where you are when it comes to trusting others and being supported.
- Take a sauna or steam bath. Sit in a Jacuzzi for a safe period of time.
- Dine at restaurants that serve the cuisine of different cultures or countries. Notice your reaction to trying different kinds of food.
- Participate in a sport you haven't experienced.
- If you like the outdoors, try hiking in a new type of terrain.
- Learn survival skills by contacting Outward Bound programs for adults. Or contact other naturalists who offer training in the wild, such as The Desert School at www.joshuatree.org, or The Boulder Outdoor Survival School at www.boss-inc.com.

If you take on one of these suggestions and have an intense emotional response or a gut feeling that you are experiencing a past life, you've been triggered. Do not continue to do the mental trigger exercises. Move ahead to the Magic Mirror Meditation. If none of these triggering suggestions appeal to you, try answering the following mental triggering questions and suggestions.

Mental Karmic Triggers

When Harvey came to my office for a past-life regression, he felt blocked. He hated his job, where he was underpaid and bored. He had been employed at the same company as a technological consultant for fifteen years and was at a dead end. There was no opportunity for advancement. However, no other company responded when he sent out his résumé.

Why did he choose a past-life regression to remedy his problem? After reading a book on regression, Harvey was triggered. Somehow he knew the process could help him release his block. Reading the book inspired him to make an appointment for a past-life regression.

As Harvey drifted into trance, his whole body began to tremble. The first image that he recalled was a clock. I asked him to zoom in on the image. He saw a portly man wearing a three-piece suit holding a pocket watch. The man had a handlebar mustache and a mean scowl on his face. He was standing on the second floor of a large factory looking down at the production area, supervising the workers. Harvey knew that he was in England in the late 1800s.

I asked Harvey how he felt about himself.

In a deep trance, Harvey observed, "I'm not a very nice person. My employees don't like me."

When I asked Harvey to experience an important incident, he said, "I'm in this large, empty house. I feel so alone. It's like I have no one. I don't have a family or anyone."

Tears welled up in Harvey's eyes as I asked him to recall his death.

"I'm an old lonely man. I'm so unhappy. It seems that all I cared about was money. It's as though I didn't believe in a higher power. I had no faith in myself outside of my ability to make money."

Harvey visualized his sadness leaving his chest by imagining a clock breaking into a thousand pieces.

When he came out of trance, he felt peaceful and surprised.

"It's not how I am in this life. I always try to help others. In fact, people call me Mr. Sunshine."

Harvey called me a month later to say that he had been fired two weeks after the regression. The day after he was fired, he got a call, from out of the blue, offering him a job doing voiceover work. This was something he had always wanted to try. He also got a response from another company, offering him more money with an opportunity for advancement, which he accepted. He shared his revelation with me.

"This time, I trust the universe to provide everything I need. I'm here to serve humanity. When I'm serving, I'll be taken care of as well. I need to love what I do, not just work for money."

Your karmic pop-ups can be triggered by something that is mentally stimulating, like a book or a movie. Written and spoken words as well as video and cinematic images can trigger a karmic pop-up. As in Harvey's case, simply reading a book about past-life regression motivated him to have a session.

Your Mental Karmic Detectors

To detect past-life memories related to your intellectual interests, answer the following questions to *retrieve* information, then write down your responses:

- Which historical eras interest you passionately? The Russian Revolution? The Golden Age of Greece? Other?

- What types of characters from movies and literature are you drawn to? Gangsters? Spies? Royalty? Write about your favorite characters.

- Which movie genres are you drawn to? Costume dramas? Thrillers? Foreign films?

- Are your interests or hobbies in some way unusual? Like fencing? Belly dancing? Martial arts? List them. List friends or associates who share the same interests. What do you learn from others who are exploring the same pursuits?

- What genre of books do you prefer? Romances? Mysteries? Erotica?

- Which historical figures interest you passionately? Are you drawn to rulers? Artists? Other? Who specifically?

- What types of television shows do you like to watch? What topics interest you the most? Love? Murder? Revenge? Other?

- What particular kinds of injustices cause you to become outraged? Cruelty to animals? Polluting the earth? Racial prejudice? Other?

If the answers to these questions reveal an insight relating to your goal, continue working with the following exercise.

Your Mental Karmic Triggers

Sometimes workshop participants are triggered as I lecture about past lives. They begin to recall a past life before I initiate the regression.

During one workshop, I was talking about a past-life story in which a village burned down. All of a sudden Nassim, a participant, started coughing uncontrollably. She seemed to gasp for air. Realizing she was having a past-life pop-up, I worked with her to release the trauma.

When I asked her what she was experiencing, she replied, "I can't breathe. The house is burning and I'm trapped."

A moment later she exhaled a sigh of relief, the coughing ceased, and she was calm. I asked her what had happened.

"I died of asphyxiation. It's odd, I've always had a fear of fire."

Mental Karmic Triggers Exercise

To bring mental past-life pop-ups into your conscious awareness, try one of these triggering techniques:

- Read books about the historical time periods that interest you. Notice your emotional responses as you are reading. Note your dreams the nights you read.
- Watch five or more movies that relate to your areas of interest. Notice your emotional responses as you are watching. Note your dreams.
- Attend historical reenactments: Renaissance fairs, Society for Creative Anachronism events, or historic theme parks. Pay attention to your reactions and be aware of arising coincidences.
- Visit archaeological museums; look at Egyptian mummies, a Fiji Islander exhibit, or other displays of artifacts from archaeological digs. Notice your responses to the artifacts.
- Pay attention when you have strong reactions to news stories, and write about them in your journal.
- Take part in celebrations of other cultures: a Native American powwow, a Chinese New Year's party, a Maypole dance.
- Notice when you are triggered by stories in this book.

If you take on one of these suggestions and have an intense emotional response or a gut feeling that you are experiencing a past life, you've been triggered. Move ahead to the Magic Mirror

Meditation. You may want to work with the flower essences on page 62 to help you be more receptive.

Fasten Your Seat Belt—Remember and Reprogram

Now that you've been triggered, you're ready to move to the next steps of the karmic healing process: remember and reprogram. Since you have practiced the visualization and relaxation techniques, you should be able to access your higher self with ease.

Here's a tip. It's going to feel strange to find yourself in a different type of body. You may be a different race or gender than you are now. If you are a petite blond female, it would be weird to experience yourself as a six-foot male. And vice versa, if you are a macho guy, it could be bizarre to see yourself as a woman wearing high-heeled shoes.

Trust your impressions. Even if you think you are making it up, go with your experience. The more you practice, the more confident you'll become with your ability to access your inner guidance.

Magic Mirror Meditation

It's best to record this meditation and play it to yourself. You may also want to play relaxing music in the background. Set aside about forty minutes to do the whole meditation. Take the first ten minutes to deeply relax. You may use a recording of the relaxation exercise from chapter 1. During the meditation, pause after each question and command to give your subconscious mind enough time to respond.

Go to your sacred space. Relax into a comfortable position, either lying down or sitting, and close your eyes.

Breathe deeply and allow yourself to melt into a feeling of peace. Do the total body relaxation exercise. Visualize being enveloped in a protective cocoon of white light. Allow your conscious mind to drift and float off.

Then imagine you're riding in a limousine, moving through space and time, to another lifetime. The limousine comes to a stop at a major movie studio. The driver opens the door and helps you out.

You enter the studio through a huge door and walk down, down, down many steps to a long corridor. A beautiful woman greets you. She escorts you down, down, down more steps into another long corridor and into a room filled with costumes. She tells you to look through them all and find one that appeals to you.

When you find the costume you want, she invites you to try it on. Look in the dressing room mirror and study the costume that you're wearing. What is it? What kind of fabric is it made from? What time period is it from? Are you a man or a woman? What color is your skin? What country are you in? What feelings, thoughts, and sensations come to you as you stand there in this costume?

Go to an important incident in this lifetime. See it happening in the mirror. What are you experiencing? Trust your impressions. Receive the information in a way that's easy and comfortable for you. What's the outcome of the incident you see?

Now go to your time of passing. View it in a way that's easy and comfortable. How did you die?

Now look into the mirror and scan that whole life, as if watching a movie on a television screen. Take note of anything you notice, any images, thoughts, or feelings that arise. What spiritual lesson did you learn from that lifetime?

What body sensations do you have? Do you feel any pain? Locate the pain or sensation in your body. Assign an image to it. How big is it? How much does it weigh? What kind of material is it made of? What color is it? How do you want to get rid of it?

Release the sensation now into the clear light of universal love. Fill your whole body with white light. Imagine this light shining down on your face. On your neck, on your torso, and all the way within you. Feel the light giving every cell of your body permission to function in perfect health. You are healing on all levels—physical, emotional, mental, and spiritual.

In just a few minutes, it will be time to return to your waking state. Mentally count from one to five. On the count of five, you'll be wide awake, and you'll remember all that you experienced.

One, coming up, get a sense of your environment. Two, coming up. Three, begin to feel your body. Four, wiggle your fingers and toes. Stretch. Five, wide awake, feeling good. Open your eyes and feel wide awake, better than before.

When you are ready, get your journal and write about this experience. Allow your thoughts to flow gently into your pen and onto the page. Trust your experience as you answer these questions:

- Did you recognize the beautiful woman who guided you?
- Did she shape-shift into something else? If so, what?
- What type of costume did you try on?
- What type of fabric was it made from?
- What time period was it from?
- Were you a man or a woman?
- What color was your skin?
- What was the year or time period?
- What country were you in?
- What important incident did you experience?
- What was the outcome?
- How did you die?
- What feelings, thoughts, and images did you experience while wearing your costume?

- What spiritual lesson did you learn?
- Did you have any body sensations or pain? If so, what?
- What image did you use to transform it?
- How does this information or story apply to your present life?

Meditation-Enhancing Flower Essences

Two drops of flower essence taken in water before practicing a meditation can aid your development. It's best to choose just one essence from the list. Work with one at a time until you get to know it. Select one of the following essences:

- **Nutmeg:** helps you access wisdom from past lives
- **Angelica:** enhances your awareness of spiritual forces
- **Lotus:** deepens your meditative experience
- **Aspen:** overcomes any fear of crossing into the spiritual dimensions

Affirmations

The third step of karmic healing—reprogramming—uses affirmations. Affirmations can help you change your limiting beliefs by replacing your negative thoughts with positive ones. You can find a negative thought by answering this question: How does your past-life story apply to your present life?

The following story shows how to turn your answer into a positive statement.

Brian was in emotional turmoil. His current girlfriend was cheating on him, but he had not been able to leave her. Something kept holding him back.

During the Magic Mirror Meditation, Brian tried on a tunic and sandals. He knew that he was in Italy and that he was married to his present-life girlfriend. A feeling of sadness overcame him when he saw himself on a ship as a crewmember. He had hired himself out on a long ship voyage, hoping to make more money to support her. At the time of his death many years later, he deeply regretted the long absence from his beloved wife. He had made the mistake of not spending more time with her.

When I asked Brian how his past-life story applied to his present life, he said, "I can't leave her."

I asked him to turn his statement into an affirmation, and he replied, "I can leave her." I recommended that he take a bleeding heart flower essence to help him release his unhealthy attachment.

A few days later, Brian called me to say that he had left his girlfriend. He was sad but glad to move on.

Follow-Up Questions

You may have received a whole story while doing the Magic Mirror Meditation. For instance, Andrew tried on a big gray beard and a big black hat. He knew that he was in Russia and that he was a patriarch. Feelings of intense joy overcame him when he saw himself sitting at a huge dining table with his family. However, when he saw himself dying of old age he felt very sad. He realized that he had wanted to hang on to the highlight of his younger days, and by doing so had missed a lot of enjoyment from being in the present moment. He visualized the sadness he felt in his heart turning into an orange butterfly and flying away.

When I asked Andrew how his past-life story applied to his present life, he said, "I have trouble letting go. I don't do well with making changes."

I recommended that he take a walnut flower essence to help him release the past and move into the future with ease. I also recommended the affirmation "It's safe for me to let go and to let in new experiences."

Not everyone is able to retrieve an entire story during the regression meditation. Some people just feel physical sensations, others feel an emotion, and some just receive an image. Here are some examples:

- During a group regression, Sandy only felt body sensations. She felt as though her body were growing larger and larger. She felt powerful and had the impression she could intimidate anyone with her size. I asked Sandy how it applied to her present life, in which she was a petite Asian woman. She said, "There are other ways to be powerful, outside of physically having to throw your weight around. I've really had to work on communicating. But I've learned to ask for what I want." I recommended that she take a vine flower essence to release her unconscious need to dominate others. I suggested that she use the affirmation "I am a powerful woman."

- Marcy's experience was very emotional. She knew that she had died giving birth. She cried through the entire meditation. When I asked her how it applied to her present life she said, "I never wanted to have children. Maybe this is the reason why." I recommended that she take a sweet chestnut flower essence to release the trauma. I suggested that she use the affirmation "I am at peace with my inner woman."

- Todd simply received an image of a plain-looking woman standing with two children. When I asked him what the image meant, he said, "Love isn't always like a romance you see in the movies. Sometimes it's just living with someone who cares for you, day to day. Also, I am proud to be a good father. I'd do anything for my boys."

If you had trouble retrieving information during the meditation, ask yourself the following questions:

- If you only received body sensations, what were they? Do they correspond to any health issues you may have? If you felt as though you were in a different body, make up a past life scenario involving that person. What positive qualities did that person have? What negative qualities did he or she have? How do the qualities apply to your life?
- If you received an emotional release, what issue does it relate to in your present life?
- If you received an image, what does it represent to you? What does it symbolize?

You don't have to receive a whole story to experience soul healing. Trust what you receive is a valid message.

Flower Essence Remedies—Reinforce

The fourth step of the karmic healing process is to *reinforce* your efforts. Now you are ready to let go of blocks and barriers and begin new ways of being. Here are several flower essences I recommend for some general conditions. You'll need to take the remedy every day for a month to keep the issue that was triggered and released in your meditation at bay. Select one of the following flower essences and follow the dosage directions on the label:

- **Bleeding heart:** releases a powerful emotional attachment to the past
- **Chestnut bud:** stops the habit of making the same mistake, encouraging the ability to learn from experience
- **Sagebrush:** releases old behaviors and responses that are no longer appropriate

- **Wintergreen:** cleanses the aura of negativity from a past experience
- **Mimulus:** brings courage and confidence to face life's challenges
- **Aspen:** releases hidden fears

Summary

You have experienced the first level of karmic healing. You have:

- **Retrieved** soul messages by completing the triggering exercises and answering the questionnaires
- **Remembered** past-life data as a story, body sensations, an image, or an emotional release by practicing the regression meditation
- **Reprogrammed** positive images into your mind by using visualization and affirmation
- **Reinforced** your work to release blocks and barriers by taking a particular flower essence

You now have established a greater connection to your soul and its wisdom. Some of you may have concerns or doubts about the information you have received. Trust the process and be patient. Once you get comfortable using your psychic senses, exploring how karma operates in your life will become irresistible. A whole new world is opening for you. You may see an immediate change, or your issue may need more work. Be persistent. You'll want to mail a copy of your commitment letter to yourself now to give you continued support.

In the next chapter, you'll discover how spiritual healing works and what to expect while undergoing the karmic healing process.

your spiritual makeover

Let's explore the karmic healing process in more detail and give you the tools to clear away your *karmic clutter*, the unwanted things that stand in the way of accessing your potential. In this chapter, you'll learn how to prevent a possible crisis in your life and make positive changes while standing at a *karmic crossroad*. We'll look at how you can reset your *karmic clock* so you'll have a better sense of timing and feel more connected to the entire cosmos. In all, you'll discover how to have a total spiritual makeover.

Your Autopilot

Many people who have come to me for readings have the same complaints: "If only he or she would commit." "If only he or she would stop drinking." "If only he or she would leave his or her unhappy marriage." If only . . . I'm sure you can fill in the blank to make an "if only" statement about someone in your life.

When looking at someone else's life, the answer to their problem often looks obvious. Apparently, the person just won't do what they need to do to heal. They won't get help. Or they adamantly refuse to change or take any good advice. In fact, sometimes the person obstinately chooses to be depressed, stuck, or blocked. It's very difficult to watch a person waste their talents or squander their resources. But sometimes people need to learn the hard way, or they may choose to not learn at all. And sometimes that person is us.

Why do people engage in destructive behaviors? The answer is simple. We have the freedom to choose how we respond to our challenges and circumstances. But most of us are not conscious of our choices. Enslaved by habitual responses, we allow circumstances to dictate the course of our life.

I'll tell you how it works. Your subconscious mind is like a tape recorder. It is continually recording your sensory perceptions along with your emotional states and mental processes. It's equipped to rewind and replay the incidents of your life. Most people spend a lot of time pressing the rewind button, thinking about the past, or they try to imagine the future. Rarely are we on *play*, in the present moment.

Here's an example. It's Friday afternoon, and you're driving down the highway. You're in a good mood, anticipating the weekend ahead. All of a sudden you see an image of a woman talking on the phone on a billboard, and you realize you forgot to send your mother a birthday card. For the next few miles, you make yourself feel bad. You say to yourself, "How could I be so inconsiderate? She's going to be mad." You recall the disaster that occurred last year when you forgot. Your good mood turns into anxiety as you frantically try to think of how you can excuse yourself for your blunder.

You become lost in your feelings and thoughts, though you're still driving. You're not giving your full attention to the road ahead. While you're living inside a replay of your memories and fantasies, who do you suppose is driving your car?

Your subconscious autopilot is driving for you. You've driven the route home so many times, you know it without paying attention to it. You've programmed your subconscious by repetition.

The same thing happens in other situations. Anytime you're not on play, you're subject to living out your subconscious mind's automatic responses. Thus you often don't make conscious choices—because you are not being present. You allow your unconscious reflexes to take over.

Karmic Crossroads

Past-life regression can make you aware of your automatic responses and can also bring an unrecognized issue into your conscious awareness. When this happens, people are presented with a choice: they can either embrace the problem and take responsibility for solving it, or they can cover it up and not deal with it. I call this choice a karmic crossroad.

My client Lucy was at a karmic crossroad. She came into my office for a reading because she suspected that her husband was cheating on her. She feared that if she confronted her husband, he might leave her and their two children. But if her life continued on the same track, she feared she'd develop ulcers or some other stress-related illness. What was worse, living with deceit and illness or risking being a single parent with integrity?

Since she was unable to truly talk to her husband, I suggested that she do a past-life regression to release her block about speaking out. Desperate to save her marriage, she agreed. However, she was skeptical of the past-life regression process. Her biggest fear was that she'd make up a story that wasn't true. I reassured her that it didn't matter and suggested that she let go of any expectations. She was surprised at what she discovered when she drifted into a deep state of relaxation.

"I see a brown-skinned hand clutching a wet rag, scrubbing a tiled kitchen floor."

Lucy knew that she had immigrated to America from the Caribbean to be a housekeeper for an old man.

"The house is quiet. I have the feeling that I am alone most of the time. I like the elegant furnishing of the house: the Oriental carpets, the brocaded sofa, and the mahogany cabinet filled with china plates. I see myself burying my face in the velvet curtains that hang from the windows. The fabric feels so silky and sensuous against my skin. I was very poor on the island. Living here seems like a dream come true."

During the regression, when I asked Lucy to move to the source of the problem with her present husband, she had a realization. Another part of her job in her past life was to service the old man's sexual needs. She began to cry.

"When I enter his room, he's waiting for me in his bed. His body revolts me, but I lie down beside him. I let him do what he wants. I resign myself to it. If I am to stay here, I must endure this."

When I asked Lucy whether she recognized the old man as anyone in her present life, she started laughing hysterically.

"It's my husband, Jim."

I coached Lucy to notice any sensations she may have been feeling in her body.

"I feel like something heavy is pushing down against my torso."

When I suggested that she assign an image to the heaviness, she imagined the sensation to be a big rock. She released the rock by throwing it away, and the pressure disappeared. I asked her to imagine a white dove in her heart, and she became filled with a deep sense of inner peace.

Then I had Lucy ask her inner guidance for a message to help her with her relationship with Jim.

Her inner voice said, "I have my place. It has its unspoken limits and duties."

In her following session, I asked Lucy whether she had uncovered her unspoken limits and duties. She shared her insights.

"All week, the similarities between my past life as a servant and my present life began to unfold. My husband works in his family's business nine to five, while I work nonstop from the moment I wake up at six until I go to bed at midnight. I teach Pilates forty hours a week, clean the house, and take care of the kids. My husband has one job, while I have three. It occurred to me that we never talked about this arrangement of responsibilities. Over the course of our ten-year marriage, we never agreed that this is how it should be. We just fell into this pattern."

I asked her what the silent expectations were.

"We have many unspoken agreements. For instance, Jim expects me to do everything around the house, but he never lifts a finger to help. When household chores don't get done in the course of the day, he gets angry. All week, I heard his silent expectations loud and clear. 'Why isn't dinner ready?' 'You forgot to take out the trash.' 'The kids have to be picked up from baseball practice.' 'The dogs need to be fed.'

"The most important thing I have noticed is my silent submission. In my past life I never spoke out to the old man. I never felt it was my place to voice my truth. I had the attitude of grin and bear it, and accept my duty.

"I haven't been able to really talk to Jim. I've never asked him to help out with the chores. I've allowed myself to be his servant. I'm even stuck in silent submission when we have sex. Usually I'm too tired, but do it anyway. I go through the motions, but don't really enjoy myself. I'm so exhausted I go numb or space out."

Over the course of a few more weeks and more healing sessions, Lucy came to the conclusion that she couldn't go on being a servant any longer. She wanted more of an equal partnership in her marriage. Her soul's yearning to grow was so strong it gave her the courage to begin sharing her insights with Jim. She asked him if he would help out with the housework and with parenting the kids.

Unfortunately, he didn't want to change. Jim liked having a servant take over his share of responsibility. Since Lucy worked all those extra hours, he had spare time to spend with his girlfriend. When Jim finally confessed that he was having an affair, Lucy filed for a divorce. She received a generous settlement and custody of the children. She went into therapy to continue to heal. The last I heard, she was enjoying being a single parent.

Lucy came to a crossroad, and she resolved to heal. She wanted a better relationship, and she was ready to work on one. However, her husband also came to that crossroad, and he did not want to change their relationship. Their divorce forced Lucy to grow emotionally. It's not what she had originally hoped would happen, but the outcome was for the good of all.

Be certain you are ready to get answers to your problems or issues, and be just as ready to have those problems or issues dissolve. When the root cause of your problem is revealed, that is your karmic connection. Transformation will occur, but only if you're ready to embrace it, only if you're willing to take responsibility for what you have uncovered.

Karmic Crossroad Meditation

You'll need to do this exercise sitting up, so you can comfortably write in your journal. You may want to record the directions so you can play them back. Go to your sacred space. Relax into a comfortable seated position, and close your eyes. Breathe deeply and allow yourself to melt into a feeling of peace. Turn on your recorder.

Your life is on a certain track with certain predictability. You have certain habits. You have a daily routine. Now imagine your life five years from now. If your life keeps going exactly the way it's been going, how will it look? If you make no changes, allowing the flow of your life to unfold as it has before, what will you be doing? If your exercise program stays the same as it is now, what will be the state of your health? If your stress level stays the same, how will it affect your well-being? If your eating habits stay the same, how will that affect your body and self-image? If you make no changes in how you relate to others, how will your relationships be functioning? What will the status of your sex life be? If you make no changes regarding your spending habits, how will your financial profile look? How much debt will you have? If the way you relate to family members doesn't change, how will your home life look? Will you come to a crossroad? Will some area of your life become so out of balance that a crisis will occur?

When you are ready, slowly open your eyes and come back into the present.

Karmic Crossroad Exercise

If your life keeps going exactly the way it's been going, how will it look five years from now? Answer the following questions:

- What will be the condition of your finances?
- What will be the condition of your health?
- What will be the condition of your body and self-image?
- What will be the condition of your family relationships?
- What will be the condition of your sex life?
- What will be the condition of your intimate relationships?
- What area(s) of your life will come to a crisis?
- What changes do you need to make to avoid a crisis?
- What actions do you need to take to avoid a crisis?
- What kind of support do you need to make the changes?
- Who do you need to enroll to support you?

Follow-Up Resources

Other people who have done this exercise reported the following discoveries:

- Georgia said that if she didn't change her heath habits, she would probably wind up like her mother, with diabetes and walking with a cane. To prevent a karmic crossroad, she signed up for a weight loss program, joined a gym, and made an appointment with an acupuncturist.
- John said that if he continued his spending sprees and maxing out his credit cards, he would be bankrupt. To prevent a karmic crossroad, he made an appointment with a financial advisor.
- Marge reported that life would be fine, but not special. She would just coast along without really fulfilling her dream to travel around the world. To prevent a karmic crossroad, she began researching travel packages on the Web, and she checked out travel books from the library.

If you're still unclear about the direction of your life, consult a form of divination. Get a tarot card reading, have an I Ching or astrology consultation, or seek advice from rune stones. The following Web sites are good sources:

- www.tarot.com/tarot/index.php
- www.tarot.com/oracle
- www.webtarot.org
- www.facade.com
- www.destinytarot.com

Karmic Crossroad Affirmations

The following affirmations can be used with taking a flower essence following your karmic crossroad visualization exercise.

Choose one that applies to your problem, and write it in your journal 108 times a day. The number 108 is considered sacred for many reasons. One is that there are 108 energy lines converging to form the heart chakra (energy center). One of these lines leads to the crown chakra and is said to be the path to self-realization.

Or you may want to post it somewhere as a reminder. Hang it on your mirror, your refrigerator, or another prominent location.

- It is safe for me to change.
- I am moving forward with ease and pleasure.
- I surrender to my higher self.
- I am willing to release the past.
- I take the actions I need to take.
- I am willing to be totally satisfied.
- I honor and nurture myself.
- I can have what I truly want.
- I am patient and persevering.

Karmic Crossroad Flower Essences

Here are some suggestions to remedy some general conditions:

- **Impatiens:** curbs overly impulsive behavior
- **Morning glory:** releases harmful personal habits
- **Cayenne:** acts as a fiery catalyst for change
- **Wild oat:** clears confusion about what you want in life
- **Hibiscus:** releases blocks to sexual desire
- **Blackberry:** helps manifest desires
- **Sagebrush:** releases cravings that hinder your growth

Getting to the Core Issue

Over the years I've worked with many people who have wanted to resolve a specific issue. In the process of karmic healing, they have discovered that what they thought was the problem wasn't really the problem at all. When they went deep into their core, they uncovered the real issue, and thereby were able to transform.

For example, my client Claire thought she had the answer to her weight problem. All she needed to do was eat less and exercise more. However, she couldn't stick to a diet. She joined a gym, but she never seemed to find the time to go there. Her live-in boyfriend constantly criticized her body, saying, "How can you look at yourself in the mirror?" He began flirting with the woman who lived next door, which enraged Claire.

The more jealous and insecure Claire became, the more weight she'd gain. Her eating habits seemed to be getting out of control, and her relationship was deteriorating. She was in turmoil, and she called me for a psychic reading. When I suggested that she have a regression session to get to the root of her problem, she was hesitant. She was afraid it wouldn't work. But she was desperate, and she scheduled an appointment.

Drifting into trance, she saw that she had a dainty cinnamon-colored hand wearing gold rings set with glimmering rubies. She had thick black hair and a perfectly shaped body adorned in a silk sari. She knew that she was in India.

When I asked Claire to go to the source of her problem, she smiled.

"I'm a dancer. I have many admirers."

But a moment later, Claire burst into tears.

"No one sees ME! I'm like an object. Men want to own me. They only want me because I'm beautiful."

While Claire was still in trance, I asked her how being overweight in her current life served her.

"I want a man to love me as a person, not for how I look."

Claire felt a deep sense of sadness and began to weep. Her grief seemed stuck in her heart like a piece of metal, and she released it by visualizing pulling out the blade of a dagger. We filled the space in her heart with a pink lacy valentine. She affirmed that she loves and accepts herself. I recommended that she take a pretty face flower essence to help her radiate her inner beauty and release her need to overidentify with her outer image.

When Claire came out of the trance, she felt and looked ten pounds lighter.

"It doesn't matter whether the story is true or not, I feel great!"

She called me a week later to tell me she left her boyfriend. "He always made me feel that I wasn't good enough. It was as though there was something wrong with me. At last I feel free to be myself."

Soon after, Claire found someone who loved her for the person she was and for whom her weight made no difference.

"He thinks I'm beautiful and always compliments me," she reported. A few years later, they married.

Claire is still overweight, but she chooses not to diet and exercise. Her anxiety about her appearance disappeared after the regression. She has come to accept and enjoy being buxom and full-figured. The important thing to her is being truly loved.

Although Claire originally thought that her real problem was her weight, she discovered that it wasn't her core issue at all. Her arguments with her ex about her extra pounds were only a symptom of a deeper problem calling to be healed. Her regression helped her connect with her true emotional need, which was being loved for her *inner* beauty. She was then free to make the changes she needed to be fulfilled.

Symptoms versus Root Causes

In our society we tend to seek and treat symptoms. If you have a headache, you take an aspirin. If you can't sleep, you take sleeping pills. Pharmaceuticals can remedy a short-term problem, but they don't necessarily provide you with a long-term solution. Often our symptoms are externalizations of deeper issues calling out to get our attention, as in Harry's case.

When medical doctors were unable to relieve Harry's chronic shoulder pain, he tried massage therapy. After a few sessions there was no improvement, so his massage therapist suggested a past-life regression. Perhaps there were emotional issues linked to the pain that a past-life regression could bring to light.

Harry was skeptical that a regression would work. But his painful shoulder was interfering with his ability to play tennis, his favorite form of recreation. After weighing his options—giving up tennis or taking a risk—he scheduled an appointment.

In my office, Harry regressed to see himself as a dark-haired man standing on the second-floor landing of a marble staircase in a huge mansion. He knew that he was a successful European businessman.

When I asked him to zero in on the cause of his problem, he began to breathe rapidly.

"I'm arguing with my business partner on the staircase. Oh my God! He has a knife."

I asked Harry what happened.

"He stabs me in the *shoulder* as I turn away."

I placed my hands on Harry's shoulder and gave him a Reiki treatment; the pain disappeared. While Harry is still in trance, I asked him to go to the outcome of the stabbing incident.

"I fall down the marble stairs and die."

I asked him to scan that life and retrieve any other important information.

"Oh my! My business partner is my lover in this life."

When Harry came out of trance, his pain was completely gone. He confided that he had been recently arguing with his lover about money.

"It's like I'm reliving the same scenario in a way. My lover has a volatile personality and is very controlling. I don't know if I can really trust him with my money."

I asked Harry what he needed to do to protect himself. He promised me that he would talk to his lawyer to learn his financial rights in his relationship. He left my office feeling like a new man.

A few weeks later, Harry called to tell me that he had reinjured his shoulder in a bicycle accident. I asked him whether he had spoken to his lawyer as he had promised. He was embarrassed to admit that he hadn't. The minute he got home after his regression, he had forgotten all about it.

Harry still felt he couldn't trust his lover. The sad part was that he still wasn't ready to trust his own intuition either. Harry was back where he started.

Using a Mantra to Connect to Your Core

A mantra is a syllable, word, or phrase in Sanskrit that elevates or modifies consciousness through its meaning, sound, and vibration. Chanting it over and over out loud or silently repeating it in your mind has great benefits.

The mantra *Sat Nam* ("saht nahm") means, "Truth is my identity, and I call upon the eternal Truth that resides in all of us." Repeated use of this mantra can clear the subconscious mind so that past wounds no longer get in the way of self-realization. Working with it will erase habitual thought patterns that do not resonate with your true essence. Chant this mantra out loud or silently in your mind 108 times a day to connect with your core of truth and awaken to your infinite identity.

Your Karmic Clock

When it comes to healing and making changes, everyone's speed of growth is different. Claire was able to make changes in her life very quickly after her session. Other people either resist or need more time to work through an issue, as my client Harry illustrates.

Many people know what they need to do to heal, yet they resist. They know what they need to do to lose weight, stop smoking, or leave a bad relationship, yet they don't take the actions. It's often because they are not truly ready to heal. The timing mechanism that controls the speed of our soul growth is our built-in *karmic clock*.

Your higher self, or your soul, knows what you truly need to heal. Some people need a crisis or a wake-up call. Harry obviously needed a chronic pain to motivate him to seek help. However, when we get the message about what we need to do and don't act, we may encounter another crisis. Harry knew he had to make a simple phone call, but he didn't. Perhaps the accident was a warning reminding him to pay attention and take care of his needs.

Here's how to realign your timing:

- Are all the clocks and watches in your home and car set on the same time? If not, set them to agree.
- Do you have any clocks that are stopped? If so, repair them or throw them away.
- Do you have a problem with being late? If so, make it a project to clean up your integrity and be on time.

Set Your Karmic Clock Meditation

This visualization will allow you to experience yourself as part of a greater whole and will connect you to the natural cycles of the cosmos. You may want to record the meditation.

Go to your sacred space. Relax into a comfortable position, lying down or sitting up with your spine straight. Close your eyes. Breathe deeply and allow yourself to melt into a feeling of peace.

Imagine that you are outside on a beautiful summer day. The sun is shining, and the air feels warm and pleasant. You are looking at a lovely garden where a variety of flowers are blooming. Some plants grow high and tall. Other plants creep along the ground. Some plants are in full bloom, while others will blossom much later. Every plant has its own rate of growth.

Birds are singing. You enjoy their songs. You know the birds will only be here for a season before they migrate. They know when to return, and they know when to leave.

The leaves on the trees are a deep green. In a few months, they will turn colors and fall to the ground.

Everything in nature has its own cycle. The sun rises and sets, as does the moon. You are part of this grand cycle. Your life is in divine order. You are one with the divine plan of your life. You feel relaxed and at ease. Tune to your own rhythm. Know that you are at one with the turning of the earth, the movements of the planets, the pulse of the stars.

Ohm is the sound of the current of love that connects the stars, the earth, the trees, the birds, the animals, the plants, all the people, everyone, everything.

Ohm. Listen to that sound. Feel the oneness. Feel the peace.

When you are ready, slowly open your eyes and come back into the room.

Ohm—The Sound of Oneness

The sound of ohm is the vibration of love that permeates the universe, connecting everyone and everything. It is the audible current of that connection. Chant the ohm mantra or listen to a recording of it, and you will feel part of a great oneness.

To find a recording of an ohm mantra, check these Web sites:

- www.ethereanmusic.com
- www.midashealth.com
- www.dicksutphen.com

Karmic Clock Affirmations

The following affirmations will help you to reprogram your karmic clock:

- I am always at the right place at the right time.
- My timing is perfect.
- I have a good sense of timing.
- I allow the divine plan of my life to manifest in perfect time in perfect ways.

Karmic Clock Flower Essences

Here are some suggestions to help reset your karmic clock:

- **Aloe vera:** revitalizes when burned out from living a fast-paced life
- **Blackberry:** creates a sense of future possibilities
- **Dandelion:** releases the compulsion to stress the body through overactivity and setting unrealistic deadlines
- **Elm:** releases feeling of being overwhelmed by events
- **Mimulus:** releases the fear that there isn't enough time for daily tasks
- **Zinnia:** releases feelings of being pressured by time
- **Impatiens:** releases the feeling that there isn't enough time

A Spiritual Overhaul

How can karmic healing bring about change in your life? When facing a karmic crossroad, you have an opportunity to let go of negative beliefs, such as fear, shame, or guilt. It's a chance to grow spiritually. It's like getting a *spiritual makeover*.

The process is similar to the fashion-makeover television shows. Everyday people who are undergoing some transition—graduating from college, having a baby, or facing a milestone birthday or anniversary—apply to be a contestant on the show.

Contestants wanting a new look consult with a team of fashion experts who own trendy clothing stores and beauty salons. The first ordeal that contestants face is their closet; they are commanded to throw away items that don't enhance their appearance. When contestants must get rid of their favorite blue jeans, they often cry or put up a struggle.

Their second ordeal is to confront their hairstyle. They often have anxiety attacks while sitting in a stylist's chair, waiting for their ponytails to be cut off.

Facing change is not easy. It's a process that is both terrifying and exciting. It's not pleasant to hear you're not accentuating your best features. It's hard to be coached, because you have to trust that the expert has a better vision for you than you do. You have to accept another point of view to expand your view of yourself.

Once contestants surrender to the process, they are pleased by the end result. The before and after photographs are amazing. Contestants usually change the way they view themselves. They feel more positive and more self-love.

Spiritual Makeover Discomfort Zone

If you have followed all the exercises so far, you may be feeling discomfort in some area. This is a critical time in your spiritual growth. Like the contestant in the stylist chair waiting for the scissors, you fear letting go of the familiar.

You may feel like some area of your life is falling apart. This is because things need to break down before they can be put back together in a better way. That may appear in your life in one of the following ways:

- You may be experiencing some kind of ailment.
- You may feel mentally overwhelmed.
- A problem in a relationship may have gotten much worse.
- You may be resisting change.
- Your life may have taken off in a new direction.

Wherever you are is perfect. But here are some tips to get you through the rough spots:

- If you are sick, get some medical treatment. But along with that treatment, investigate a holistic cure. Examine the belief systems related to your illness. A great guide that associates the body with its psychological counterparts is *You Can Heal Your Life*, by Louise Hay.
- If you are overwhelmed, take more downtime for yourself. You need more time to integrate the changes you're making. Don't overschedule. Take extra time for healing activities—relaxing baths, walks in nature, meditation, and so on.
- If your relationship issue has worsened, it's been amplified to show you what isn't working. Let the old ways of relating die and then re-create a new contract. You are on the verge of a tremendous breakthough. Do whatever you can to upgrade your integrity.
- If you are resisting change, get support from a friend to put you back on track. If you haven't picked up this book in over a month, you've fallen off track. Be persistent. You are on the verge of transformation.
- If your life has taken off, take a little break before moving to the next chapter.

Karmic Clutter

Unfortunately, you can't take before and after photographs of a spiritual makeover because the process happens internally. For a spiritual makeover, you release unwanted emotional patterns and limiting beliefs before you throw away your old wardrobe of ratty t-shirts or outdated suits that no longer enhance your self-image. These old patterns, and really anything you have outgrown but continue to hang on to, are your *karmic clutter*.

If you face the challenge and release your karmic clutter, you come out a better person. Blockages dissolve and new energy pathways open. The more pathways you open, the more you become aligned with your soul. The more alignment you have with your soul, the more you experience joy, bliss, and peace.

As you remove a blockage, you undergo a purification process that happens on many levels. Any time you give up a bad habit or negative belief, you begin to detoxify your soul. Sometimes the release period takes weeks to bring about change and integration. During this time of changing patterns, you may experience discomfort in the form of withdrawal. You may feel mentally confused, spacey, or overly emotional. As you adapt to the change, you may even get sick, such as coming down with a cold, as a way of coping with your temporary identity crisis.

When you change a limiting belief about yourself, you may have to let go of friends or other relationships threatened by the power of your new identity. Or you may make other changes in your life. Sometimes people relocate or make career moves.

The cosmic chain of events can go like this: One day, I bought a beautiful stained-glass rose to hang in the bathroom window. Before I could hang it up, I needed to clean the window. Then I had to get new curtains, because the old ones no longer worked with the new decor. Now the window looked fabulous, but the rest of the bathroom seemed shabby. It needed to be repainted. What started out as a simple change at the window led to a total bathroom redo. That is how change happens in your life as well. Clearing up one issue will trigger other issues to heal and transform.

On the other hand, you may want to resist change. I work out regularly with a personal trainer. After a session I always feel grounded and strong, and I have more energy. In spite of knowing how good it makes me feel, sometimes before a session I think, "I don't feel like going." Or sometimes my mind lies and says, "Working out doesn't do me any good." A part of me resists exercise, encouraging my old limiting belief that I'm helpless.

Some people do not have any withdrawal symptoms. Their lives take off in a positive way after releasing an old pattern. They have their foot on the gas pedal, smoothly accelerating into new experiences.

Releasing Physical Karmic Clutter Exercise

When I had a consultation with a practitioner of feng shui, the ancient Chinese healing practice of aligning the life force energy in your home with the earth's energy flow, I learned that one's home reflects one's inner world. The condition of your house mirrors the condition of your psyche.

Look at your own external environment. It can give you a clue as to what's going on with you internally. For example, do you hang on to objects that you don't need, can't use, or may not even like? This will help you discover what you need to do to progress.

Take an inventory of what you have:

- Are you a pack rat?
- Do you let things pile up to the point where your living space is so cluttered that it's hard to walk around without bumping into things?

- Are those unread magazines and books that are piling up around your bed acting like a protective fence?
- Do you have reminders for outdated events hanging on your bulletin board?

Open your garage door, go into your attic, or venture into your basement:

- Are you ever going to refinish those retro end tables you inherited from your aunt?
- Will you ever watch those VHS tapes now that you have a new DVD entertainment center?
- Will you ever get that lamp repaired, since its model has been discontinued and the replacement parts are no longer available?
- Will you ever use those cans of paint that are almost empty?
- Are you holding onto old computer equipment or other outdated technologies?

The clothes you haven't worn in five years that are still hanging in your closet take up both physical and psychic space. Open your closet door:

- Are you hanging on to clothes that are out of style?
- Do you still have outfits from when you were ten pounds lighter, which no longer fit?
- Are you keeping that t-shirt your boyfriend gave you because you're sentimental?

Keeping food that has outlived its expiration date is unhealthy. Open your refrigerator and cupboard doors:

- Can you find anything stale, spoiled, or past its sell-by date?

Keeping medicines that have outlived their expiration dates is also unhealthy. Open your medicine cabinet door:

- Can you find anything past its sell-by date?

Go through your computer files and cabinet files:

- Can you find anything very outdated?

If you answered yes to any of the inventory questions, I suggest that you take stock of what you have, and then let go of what you don't really need. Getting rid of old items makes way for new objects and experiences to enter. Moving twenty-one things in your living space can change the energy flow in your house to bring in fresh opportunities.

Releasing Emotional and Mental Karmic Clutter Exercise

If your space is cluttered with junk, your life is probably filled with chaos, confusion, and disorder. Hanging on to people who are unreachable is also karmic clutter and will block you from forming new potential friendships. Update your address book and email addresses. Make a point to reconnect and reestablish old ties or let them go.

The condition of your car also mirrors the condition of your psyche and possibly how well you maintain your health. Take a look at your car:

- Do you keep your car maintained and running smoothly?
- Are you in constant fear that it will break down?
- Do you keep it littered with trash?
- Does it need a trip to the car wash?

Neglecting your responsibilities on the material plane can block you from achieving your goals. Take a look at your house:

- Does your house need repair?
- Do you have a leaky roof?
- Do your walls need a new coat of paint?

- Is there a problem with the plumbing?
- What needs to be upgraded or repaired?

Unfinished tasks can block you from moving ahead. Being incomplete leaks energy and drains your vitality. Do you start things and never finish them? Make a list of projects in your house or apartment that are incomplete. Schedule time to finish them, or throw them away.

Purification Ritual

Objects can be reminders of the past, thus preventing you from moving forward. After ending a relationship, it's good to take stock of the things you've accumulated together and reassess what you really need. If you can't use an item, let it go. Have a garage sale, or give it to charity. Hanging on to things that you don't need or use just supports clutter, confusion, and attachment.

If you choose to keep items from a past relationship, it's good to spiritually cleanse them. The Native Americans use bundles of dried sage to smudge, or purify, objects, people, or even the space in a room.

You can cleanse items from the past by performing the following ritual. You'll need the following items:

- A smudge stick (available at new age bookstores or holistic supermarkets)
- An ashtray or large seashell to collect the ashes
- Matches or a lighter
- A feather to fan the smoke

Find a quiet space. Place your items in front of you. Follow the following simple steps:

- Light one end of the sage bundle.
- When it catches fire, begin fanning the smoke.

- Bathe your objects in the smoke for a minute or so.
- Fan the smoke toward you, into your aura, to clear your personal energy field.

Enjoy the feeling of clarity. You can use smudging any time you need to release negative feelings from an object, a room, or your own energy field.

Spiritual Makeover Flower Essences

Here are some suggestions to help you in your spiritual makeover process:

- **Star tulip:** enhances receptivity in meditation
- **Sagebrush:** releases that which is no longer essential to your destiny
- **Self-heal:** balances and regenerates during the cleansing and healing process
- **Easter lily:** purifies sexual desires and organs
- **Holly:** releases negative emotions such as jealousy, envy, and hostility
- **Yerba santa:** releases deep and hidden emotional toxins

Summary

By now you are in the midst of a major spiritual renovation, and I hope you are excited about your makeover. Acknowledge yourself for being courageous, persistent, and brilliant. You've learned how to take control of your life without needing a crisis to motivate you into action. Now that you know how to reset your karmic clock, you can stay in sync with your natural rhythms and cycles.

In the next chapter, I'll show you how the balancing effect of karma can play out in our lives in a host of fascinating ways.

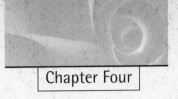

Chapter Four

Healing Your Karmic Patterns

This chapter shows how unresolved soul issues can influence your present-life *scripts*. Such unresolved issues can appear as blockages, and they can affect you physically, mentally, emotionally, and spiritually. Issues can manifest as chronic health problems, self-destructive attitudes, guilt, or the compulsive need to overcompensate in some area. I'll show you how to discover them through exercises and meditations. Once you've identified how unresolved issues are operating in your life, you'll learn how to release and resolve them.

Karmic Patterns

You've heard that cliché "You can't take it with you." It's true that when you die, you'll leave your possessions behind. You'll say good-bye to all those things you worked so hard to acquire—your car, your home, and even your flat-screen television. Worse, you'll leave your family and friends behind as well. But there are some things you do take with you.

You keep your skills and abilities, so you may be reborn with certain gifts and talents. Did you ever notice that some children are mechanically inclined, while others have a natural aptitude for math or music? Some children are outgoing, while others work much better alone. How else can you explain child prodigies, except to say that their souls have worked on one specific talent for many lifetimes.

You also keep your qualities of character, for you've earned them. I'm sure you've heard someone who is naturally kind, compassionate, and wise referred to as an old soul. Those who have been around the cosmic block a few times have worked to develop those qualities. An old soul is aware of a bigger picture.

On the other hand, people who are motivated by greed, lust, and power to control others will not find true fulfillment. They can't see a bigger picture; only their selfish desires are important to them. However, the karma generated by indulging in those pursuits will carry into a future lifetime.

The law of karma states "As you sow, so shall you reap." You will amass the consequences of everything you have done in the past, both mistakes and triumphs. At the end of your life, you will feel proud of your accomplishments, grateful for all your relationships, and happy to have made a contribution to the world. You will take that karma with you. Conversely, your regrets, unfulfilled dreams, and unresolved relationship issues will also go with you.

It is important to live your life to the fullest. It is also essential to clean up your act and restore your integrity in any area where it has faltered. It's equally crucial to forgive others for hurting you and to settle any outstanding dispute now, because it doesn't get any easier the next time around.

Along with our abilities and character, we bring our unresolved experience into each incarnation. This baggage falls into four distinct scripts, which I call *karmic patterns.* Each karmic pattern can affect us either physically, emotionally, mentally, or spiritually. Here is a brief description of the karmic patterns:

- **Body baggage:** physical symptoms remaining in the body's cell memory from past lives that affect your present health
- **Guilt quilts:** emotional remnants carried over from past lives that function as false security blankets, covering truth and thereby masking potentially positive choices
- **Fate filters:** decisions made in past lives that limit your current belief systems and subsequent actions
- **Scale balancers:** extreme actions in other lifetimes that sometimes result in overcompensation in this life

Body Baggage

Over the years, I've helped people heal chronic pains and health problems through the regression process. Mind you, past-life regression is *not* a substitute for medical treatment. In fact most people who experience a healing after a regression do so unexpectedly. They did not seek out a regression to cure an ailment.

When a physical healing spontaneously occurs during the regression process, I've found the client usually does one of the following things: recalls a violent episode involving abuse or rape, releases an injury or traumatic death, or lets go of unresolved issues of regret or betrayal that were present at the time of an earlier death.

When people experience a past-life scenario with one of those components, they usually experience pain in their body linked to a present-day illness. When they awaken from the trance, the pain disappears. Their present-day problem totally heals within a matter of weeks. Physical symptoms linked to past-life injuries or traumas are *body baggage*.

For example, Judy came to a past-life regression workshop because she was curious to find out more about herself. She had no idea that the experience would clear up her chronic problem with migraine headaches.

The weather wasn't conducive to venturing out at the time of the workshop. It was a cold, snowy night in the middle of winter, so only a few people attended. However, the warm, cozy atmosphere inside made it easy for everyone who did come to relax.

In the regressed trance state, Judy immediately traveled to France during the time of the French Revolution. She knew that she was a man and that she was involved in politics in some way.

When she was guided to view her death, she was surprised at what she experienced.

"I am standing in a line outside in a public square. The sky is gray and gloomy. A huge crowd of people, who are jeering, surrounds us. I hear the blade of the guillotine hit its mark. The crowd cheers. There are only a few more people in front of me before it's my turn to meet my death."

When I saw that Judy was experiencing a crisis, I encouraged her to view the situation in a way that was easy and comfortable. Judy began to breathe rapidly.

"I am angry, for I am innocent. They have betrayed me. I shouldn't be here! I'm innocent!"

Suddenly, a pain in her head replaced all her images and thoughts.

I asked everyone to visualize a white healing light encompassing his or her being. I affirmed that all of their cells were functioning in perfect harmony and creating perfect health.

When Judy emerged from the regression, minutes later, she was eager to share her experience with the group. Her headache had disappeared, and she felt fine. I recommended that she take a self-heal flower essence to help her restore and recover.

She said, "It's odd that I've always had sympathy for people who were unfairly cast as scapegoats."

Judy called me a month later to tell me that she hadn't had a migraine since the regression. She previously had at least two a week. Before the regression, prescription painkillers had been her only relief. Now she was pain free.

Judy experienced her karmic pattern in the form of body baggage. When she released the unresolved feelings of anger and betrayal that were present at the time of her traumatic death, her present-life pain cleared up.

Retrieve Body Baggage Issues Exercise

Give yourself an hour to complete the entire exercise. Begin the karmic healing process by taking the first step, retrieve. To see whether your health problems may be linked to unresolved soul issues, follow this exercise:

- List any chronic health problems or ailments that doctors have been unable to heal.
- Write down the areas where you hold the most tension in your body.
- List any surgical procedures you've had.
- List any physical scars, birthmarks, or handicaps you have.
- List any injuries you have suffered.
- List any areas of your body that are pierced or tattooed.
- Take note if you see a pattern forming. Is one area of your body weak, subject to illness?

Karma Cleaner Meditation

In this section, you will take the second karmic healing step, remembering. A guided meditation and drawing will help you let go of blocks and barriers related to your body. Start with the drawing by doing the following:

- Draw a basic outline of a human body on a piece of paper. It doesn't have to be perfect. It can look like a gingerbread cookie.

- Make three photocopies.
- Label two of the copies with the word "front." Label two of the copies with the word "back."
- You will also need colored pencils, felt-tip pens, or crayons.

Make a tape recording of the following script. When you are ready, go to your sacred space. Lie down in a comfortable position and turn on the tape recording.

Take a few deep breaths to center yourself. Close your eyes and go within. Draw an imaginary line cutting your body in half at your waistline. Take note of the upper half of your body. How is it energetically different than the lower half? Be a gentle observer, with no judgment. Do you feel any tightness? Do you see any colors? Does your energy feel free flowing, or do you feel it blocked somewhere?

Now erase that imaginary line. This time, with your eyes still closed, imagine a vertical line cutting your body in half from front to back. How does the front side feel compared to the back? Is it heavier? Lighter? Do you feel any tightness? Do you see any colors? Does your energy feel free flowing, or do you feel it blocked somewhere?

Erase that imaginary line. Scan your entire body, all the way from your toes up to the top of your head. Notice any colors or sensations that you feel. Scan all of your internal organs. Scan your muscles and your bones. Place your awareness on any injuries. What do you feel? Place your awareness on any scars. Do you notice any abstract shapes? Are you aware of any words or thoughts?

Take a moment to just relax. When you are ready, slowly open your eyes and come back into the room. You will remember all that you experienced.

Now retrieve one of the drawings of a human body that you labeled "front" and one labeled "back." Using your colored pens, markers or crayons, color what you experienced. Begin with your front. When you scanned the front of your body did you notice any of the following?

- Colors and abstract shapes
- Words or thoughts
- Images, such as bullet holes, shackles, or head dresses

If so, draw them. Also, try to draw any bodily or sensory experiences, for example:

- If you experienced any tightness or pain, what color was the tightness or pain? Did it have a shape? Draw the color and shape.
- Did you experience any area in your body that seemed to feel blocked? If so, draw the block. Give it a shape, color, and location. Get a sense of the size. Get a sense of the density. Color it as dark and dense or, perhaps, fuzzy and light.
- If you felt that your body was filled with energy, draw its color and direction of the flow.
- Draw how the energy from the right side differed from the left side.
- Draw how the energy of the top half of your body differed from the bottom.
- What was the energetic condition of your internal organs? Did they seem dark and heavy or bright and vibrant? Draw any quality you noticed.
- How did any operations, scars, or surgeries appear to you? Draw their shape and color.
- What was the energetic quality of your muscles and bones? Draw anything you noticed.

Now repeat this process, making a drawing for the back side of your body. When you are finished, study your drawings carefully.

How does the front differ from the back? What do they seem to say about your body?

Reprogram Your Body Baggage Meditation

Now record the following meditation. Once again, lie down and play your recording.

Close your eyes. Know that you are immersed in a sea of healing energy that is flowing all around you. Take a moment to visualize this healing energy as a golden light. Experience it entering the top of your head. Allow it to travel down your face, through your neck, and down your torso. Bathe every cell with light.

Feel this radiant light extending down your arms and into your hands. See it moving down your legs and into your feet. Experience this golden light, like rays of sunshine, filling you with vitality. Drink in this healing light. Soak it up as if you are a sponge.

Your body and mind are moving into greater harmony and greater balance. Allow every cell of your body to function in perfect harmony. Feel a deep sense of peace. You are healing on many levels. Your body is healing. Your emotions are healing. Your spirit is healing. Take as much time as you need to bathe in this delicious energy.

When you are ready, scan your body and sense any changes in your energy. Note any adjustments.

Slowly open your eyes and come back into the room.

Body Baggage Affirmations

Place the second copy of your blank drawings of "front" and "back" in front of you. Now that you've done the body baggage healing meditation, have you experienced any shifts in energy? Make a new drawing for the front and back. Now compare your first set of drawings with the second set:

- How have they changed?
- How are they the same?
- What do they say about you?

Select an affirmation from the list below to reinforce your healing. Or make up your own:

- My beauty increases every time I look in the mirror.
- I am becoming stronger and more flexible each day.
- I take good care of myself.
- I am creating perfect health.
- I am healing on all levels.
- I am healthy and beautiful.

Body Baggage Flower Essences

Use your affirmation in conjunction with one of the following flower essences to release negative patterns and imprint new positive images into your mind:

- **Crabapple:** releases obsessions with bodily impurities or imperfections
- **Arnica:** releases trauma and shock after physical injury
- **Hound's tongue:** lightens the heaviness associated with weight gain
- **Borage:** helps lift a heavy heart
- **Fuchsia:** helps alleviate physical symptoms resulting from emotional repression
- **Self-heal:** integrates the body and mind in the recovery process
- **Pretty face:** releases the fear of rejection due to personal appearance

State your affirmation each time you take your flower essence. Take two drops of the essence, four times a day. You can repeat this exercise as often as you like. Each time you'll have different insights. Every time will be a unique experience. However, stick with using the same affirmation and flower essence for at least a month.

Guilt Quilts

We are here on earth to learn and gain experience. Through the learning process, we all make mistakes. It's human to mess up. However, if we don't take responsibility for a mistake, we usually feel guilt. The guilt moves into our autopilot, where it crystallizes into fear. We then unknowingly take on that fear as an automatic response to life.

Sometimes people are blocked from moving ahead because they feel guilty about a past deed or action. However, they don't always recall what that deed was. Have you ever caught yourself saying, "What did I ever do in a past life to deserve this?"

I've found that the problem is usually not the act that was committed. Rather, the problem stems from the story we've made up around the act combined with a guilty feeling. The emotional remnants carried over from past lives that cover up the truth are *guilt quilts*.

During a group regression, Susan lay on the sleeping bag she'd carried to class. The lights were lowered, and the soothing sounds of Tibetan singing bowls filled the room. After a few minutes of listening to my slow, hypnotic voice, she slipped into a trance. Images appeared in her mind's eye. Susan knew that she was in Victorian England.

"I am wearing a white nightgown, lying on a four-postered bed. I seem to be very ill with pneumonia. My six children are at my bedside. I don't want to die! How can I leave them?"

As Susan lay on her back in the dark classroom, tears streamed down her cheeks.

When I guided the group to scan their entire past life with their soul awareness, Susan had a revelation.

"I feel guilty about dying and leaving my children. But I didn't abandon them! I didn't get sick on purpose! I can now see that my kids needed to experience losing me for their own learning and spiritual growth."

When the classroom lights went back on, Susan was the first one to raise her hand to reveal her regression to the class. The first thing she shared was how surprised she was by her emotional reaction. She had no idea where the tears had come from. She also shared her insight.

"I don't have children in this life, for I never wanted them. I used to joke 'I must have been a terrible mother in a past life' as a way to explain how strongly I felt. But now I see I wasn't terrible at all."

At the time of her previous death, Susan judged herself. Her erroneous belief that she had done something wrong by dying created a *guilt quilt*. Susan was left with an inexplicable fear of having children in this lifetime. During her past-life regression, Susan was able to release her fear and sadness, remove her quilt, and heal her guilt. When she left the workshop, she felt that it was really all right for her to forgo motherhood.

Retrieve Guilt Quilt Issues Exercise

One of the main principles of karmic healing is to be accountable for your actions. It's very simple. If you have integrity, you have a solid foundation on which to build your life. If such honor is lacking, you will suffer. The following exercise will help you begin to pinpoint where you need to upgrade and restore your integrity:

- Take responsibility and clean up any areas where you have broken agreements. In what areas of your life are you avoiding doing what you've said that you would do? At home? With money? At work? With your health? In certain relationships? What commitments haven't you fulfilled?

- Make a list of how you are breaking your commitments to yourself. Are you cheating on your diet? Are you prompt or are you always late? Are you putting off something that you know needs your immediate attention? Where can you restore your integrity with yourself? Do so immediately.

- Have you hurt someone and need to apologize? If you want that person back in your life, phone him or her and say you are sorry. If the person is dead or unreachable, write a letter of apology to him or her. Then burn it in your kitchen sink or fireplace.

- Are you holding on to borrowed possessions? Do you have overdue library books? Do you owe an outstanding debt to someone that you've been neglecting to pay back? Are you maxing out your credit cards and going deeper into debt? Do what you need to do to get back on track.

- Support others in keeping their agreements with you. If you keep company with people who lack integrity, you won't receive much support.

- If you have done something wrong, first do what you can to clean up your mistake. Then apologize to the divine spirit. Promise never to repeat your mistake. To show you are sincere, give up something for a specific time or do acts of service. Fast for a day or tithe your money to a charity. Volunteer your spare time at a shelter for the homeless or join a clean-up committee for your local park.

If you take action on your lists, your life will change in a positive manner. Your character will strengthen, and you will become trustworthy. Your reputation will grow as someone who is reliable, honorable, and dependable.

Remember Your Guilt Quilts

The guilt quilt pattern is the hardest pattern to confront. Sometimes our guilt stems from the story we've made up in our minds around an incident. However, sometimes our guilt stems from behaving badly.

It takes courage to look at our mistakes. In this process we face our pettiness, bad choices, and our lower selves. However, by meeting these unpleasant parts of our personalities, we have a great opportunity to grow. When we clean up mistakes we restore our integrity and become whole. The process forces us to have compassion as we face our own humanity, and as a result, we expand our ability to be sympathetic. The following meditation is designed to view a guilt quilt as a detached observer, so you can review a pattern objectively.

Go to your sacred space. Relax into a comfortable position and close your eyes. Breathe deeply and allow yourself to melt into a feeling of peace. Do the total body relaxation exercise. Still your mind and experience total relaxation. Surround yourself with a white light of protection.

Imagine yourself in your favorite chair sitting in front of a large screen television. You are feeling very relaxed, and at peace. In your hand you hold a remote control. In what area of your life is a guilt quilt in operation?

Press the top button on the remote control. When you press the button, an image of a past life appears on the TV screen. You can view it in a way that's easy and comfortable. What time period is it? What country is it? Are you male or female? What color is your skin? Is there anyone with you? If so, do you recognize that person from your present life? Who are the characters? What are they doing? Trust your impressions.

If you can't see an image, what are you sensing? Allow yourself to experience the heart of the issue. What body sensations are you

*feeling? What thoughts are flowing in your mind? What are the
details of the story? View it as a detached observer, as if watching
a movie. Ask your higher self, what do you need to do to heal?*

*Imagine a golden light filling every cell of your body with radi-
ance, like the golden light of the sun. It fills you with warmth and
vitality. Stay bathed in light for as long as you wish.*

*When you are ready, to come back, imagine pressing the remote
control button to turn the television off. Slowly open your eyes.*

Write down all of what you experienced. It may not even
make sense; that's okay. Record all of the images, thoughts, body
sensations, and insights.

Release Guilt Quilts

Guilt quilts have a strong emotional component. If the meditation has brought some uncomfortable emotions to surface, here
are some creative ways to encourage a cathartic release and
thereby feel better:

- Either solo or in a group, drumming helps to express and
  release buried feelings. You can find drumming circles
  nationwide at www.geocities.com/talkingdrumpub/drum-
  mingcircles.html.
- Either solo or in a group, free-form dancing can release
  feelings you may not be able to express in words. You can
  locate dance workshops at www.ravenrecording.com or
  www.groupmotion.org.
- Painting and sculpting can also be very therapeutic. Check
  with your local community centers or area colleges for
  adult classes.

Reprogram Your Guilt Quilts

If you feel guilty because you've strayed off your spiritual path,
don't worry. You can get back on it with a code of conduct the

sages used that still applies today. Avoid the seven deadly sins, qualities considered to deaden your spiritual senses and darken your inner light:

- **Pride:** excessive belief in your own abilities, which interferes with recognizing the grace of the divine. Some traditions refer to this as ego.
- **Envy:** resentment toward the good that others receive. If you are envious of another, you are telling yourself that you don't have the power to create what you need in your own life.
- **Gluttony:** an inordinate desire to consume more than what you require
- **Lust:** an inordinate craving for the pleasures of the body without the responsibility of sustaining a relationship built on love and affection
- **Anger:** an extreme dissatisfaction that can destroy relationships, families, or even countries. However, repressed anger is equally dangerous, as it can lead to health problems.
- **Greed:** the desire to acquire more wealth than you need
- **Sloth:** the avoidance of physical or spiritual work

The ancient ones had remedies, or antidotes, called the seven virtues. Practice these qualities daily:

- **Humility:** See yourself as you truly are and don't compare yourself to others.
- **Kindness:** Always behave with consideration, attention, friendliness, and sympathy to others
- **Abstinence:** Accept your body's natural limits.
- **Chastity:** Practice self-control; learn to be vulnerable with another person, to transform lust into intimacy.
- **Patience and Compassion:** Walk the path of nonviolence; act lovingly to yourself as well as toward others.

- **Temperance:** Take nothing that does not belong to you. Unearned rewards can bring unwanted obligations; find contentment with what you have.
- **Diligence:** Be disciplined, conscientious, and committed in your efforts.

When you transform deadly sins into virtues, your soul light will shine much brighter. You'll feel happier and peaceful, and thereby have more energy to accomplish greater things.

Guilt Quilt Affirmations

Select an affirmation from the list below that can reinforce your emotional healing. Or make up your own:

- I totally love and accept myself.
- I practice love and kindness.
- I practice patience and acceptance.
- I forgive myself.
- I release all anger and disappointment and go forth in happiness.
- I keep my word.

Guilt Quilt Flower Essences

Use your affirmations in conjunction with one of the following flower essences to release guilt and imprint new positive images into your mind:

- **Pine:** releases self-blame and a habit of being too hard on oneself
- **Elm:** develops an honest assessment of one's abilities
- **Mullein:** helps discern right from wrong
- **Buttercup:** releases feelings of worthlessness
- **Cherry plum:** releases the fear of losing control

- **Alpine lily:** releases shame about female sexuality
- **Agrimony:** stops covering pain and shame with a cheerful mask

State your affirmation each time you take your flower essence. Take two drops of the essence, four times a day. Stick with using the same affirmation and flower essence for at least a month.

Fate Filters

Your mind is a machine that thinks over fifty thousand thoughts a day. It chatters on and on throughout the day, making judgments, comments, and decisions. It's the voice in your head that is probably saying, "What voice is she talking about?"

As we go through life, we develop opinions and beliefs about the world and who we think we are. If a child is constantly told he is no good, he will probably grow up believing he is worthless. If he accepts the repeated negative thought, it will become part of his autopilot.

The result is that his outer life will reflect this negative thought in some way. His automatic responses will dictate the choices he makes. If he doesn't really believe he deserves wealth, he probably won't make a lot of money. His physical appearance may appear to be shoddy. People won't truly value and respect him.

If you believe you are no good, you probably lack confidence. You may also lack motivation and determination because you don't really think you can get what you want. Of course, you aren't conscious of these negative thoughts that are creating a negative condition in your life.

Your thoughts crystallize into an invisible filtering system through which you perceive the world. This filtering system is a *fate filter*. Your fate filter colors your perceptions, even though you are unaware of it. For example, you ever tried on a pair of rose-colored glasses? They make everything appear brighter at first, but after wearing them for a while, your eyes perceive the rosy appearance as normal. When you take off the glasses, it takes a while for your eyes to adjust back to their natural vision.

We create fate filters when we make decisions about who we are and how we should be in life, unknowingly programming them into our autopilot. Decisions we've made in childhood can affect our filters. Sometimes the filters are leftovers from previous lives. When people become aware of the fate filters that are holding them back, they are free to choose another way of being and thereby move forward.

Jennifer hated her job as an ill-paid secretary. Her job offered no opportunity for advancement, but she needed the security of a weekly paycheck. Since she didn't know what kind of career she really wanted to have, she had no clue as to how to go about improving her situation. When she saw past-life regression being discussed on a talk show, she was inspired. She wasn't sure how recalling a past life could help her change her life, but she was intrigued. She researched past-life regression on the Internet, found my Web site, and called me for an appointment.

During her session, I asked her to move to the source of her problem. While under hypnosis, Jennifer zoomed to a lifetime in New York City. She knew that it was during the early 1900s.

"I am wearing a drab, long-sleeved dress. It seems that I work in a factory as a seamstress. It's a kind of sweatshop. But I'm glad to be working. There's no real option except to marry someone I don't really love.

Jennifer began to cry as she continued to recall more information.

"I'm standing at an altar wearing a plain wedding gown. I feel very depressed."

While under hypnosis, Jennifer located her depression as a ball of lead in her stomach. She visualized it beaming up into a flying saucer, thus releasing it. We affirmed that she was a powerful woman who has many choices.

As she came out of her regressed state, Jennifer was slightly shocked. She said, "Oh my God! My life is exactly the same now! I hate my job. I was even considering marrying a man I don't love, just for diversion. I just play it safe."

Jennifer saw that she had always been afraid to take a chance. She never considered having a job she loved as a real possibility. At last she was ready to let go of her fate filter, "I just play it safe," and take some healthy risks. I recommended that she take a wild oat flower essence to help her on her career path together with the affirmation "I am free to assert myself." Upon using them over the course of a few months, she discovered that what she really loved was helping people. She called to tell me that she was applying to nursing school.

Retrieve Fate Filter Issues Exercise

Once you discover your unconscious limiting beliefs, you can change them. To get in touch with fate filters constructed in the past, answer the following questions:

- Are you plagued by worry and racing thoughts?
- Do you say one thing, though you are feeling the opposite?
- Are you so afraid of being criticized that you fail to assert yourself?
- Do you need the approval of others to the extent that you fail to be authentic?
- Do you always find good reasons for why you can't have what you want?

- Are you pessimistic, always seeing gloom and doom?
- Do you fail to tell the truth out of fear of not looking good?

Fate Filter Meditation

Now we'll take the insights you've received from the exercise to the next step. Remember that this meditation will help you locate and transform any fate filter that may be influencing your feelings and decisions.

Before you begin this meditation, make a tape recording of the script. When you are ready to do the exercise, go to your sacred space. Lie down in a comfortable position and turn on the tape recorder. Allow about fifteen minutes to do the meditation.

Take a few deep breaths to center yourself. Close your eyes and go within. Allow all your thoughts to drift away like feathery clouds in a blue sky. Call upon the presence of your higher self. You feel bathed in a sea of love. A deep sense of peace and relaxation fills your entire being. While in this state, you feel centered and calm. You can see yourself clearly and objectively.

Are you ready to let go of a fate filter? Take a deep breath, and trust the response you receive. Accept the answer that floats into your mind. If the answer is yes, continue. If it's no, try this again at a later time.

What negative thought about yourself are you ready to release? Take a deep breath, and trust the response you receive. Accept the answer that floats into your mind.

Where do you feel this negative thought in your body? Take a deep breath. Allow your awareness to move to those places in your body where this thought resides. Feel the sensations. Notice whether you are experiencing any feelings of tightness ... heaviness ... discomfort ... or pain.

Are there any emotions connected to this negative thought?

Breathe deeply. Allow the feelings to gently bubble up to the surface. Trust what comes.

How does this negative thought impact your life? Take a deep breath. Recall any situations in which this negative thought was present. What people interact with you when you are thinking this negative thought? What conversations do you have? How do you posture your body while this thought takes over? Allow your responses to simply flow into your mind. Trust the information that flows easily into your awareness.

Now let that all go. Feel your body. You may want to stretch. When you are ready, slowly open your eyes. Write down what you experienced in your journal.

Collage Away Karma

Now you will take the information you gathered from the meditation and turn it into a collage. Gather from magazines or newspapers a minimum of twenty-five pictures that express your fate filter. Find images that express the thought; body sensations, emotions, and situations associated with it; conversations associated with it; and people connected to it. Arrange these images on a blank page in your journal or use a larger sheet of paper. Glue the images however you like. You can add printed words. Try not to think about it; just have fun. Your completed picture is your fate filter.

Fate Filter Affirmations

Now transform your negative fate filter into a life-affirming statement. Select an affirmation from the list on the following page to reinforce your healing. Or make up your own. Your new fate filter thought should make you feel excited about the possibilities for your life. Write your positive thought in your journal, using large letters for emphasis.

- I choose to be peaceful and calm.
- I am gentle and loving with myself.
- I take time to rest and restore myself.
- I respect others and others respect me.
- I am willing to be totally honest with myself.
- I share myself with ease and confidence.

Use your affirmations in conjunction with one of the following flower essences to release negative thoughts and imprint new positive images into your mind:

- **Vervain:** releases the need to be right, regardless of the cost
- **White chestnut:** releases obsessive thoughts and worries
- **Black-eyed Susan:** counteracts denial and increases honesty with oneself
- **Snapdragon:** releases the tendency to be verbally abusive
- **Beech:** releases the tendency to be critical of oneself and others
- **Aspen:** releases anxieties and unconscious fears
- **Olive:** relieves mental and physical exhaustion.

State your affirmation each time you take your flower essence. Take two drops of the essence, four times a day. Continue to use the same affirmation and flower essence for at least a month.

Scale Balancers

The world is full of injustice. Did you ever wonder why some people achieve super stardom while others who are equally talented remain unrecognized? Why is it that some children die at an early age, before they have a chance to live a full life? And how is it that some criminals get off scot-free, while innocent people are locked up behind bars?

On a more personal level, you may have asked yourself at one time or another, "Why did my boss give a raise to someone who was less qualified than me?" "How could my lover dump me for someone not as good as me?" Or, "Why is it that I have to work so hard for everything I have while others seem to have all the luck?"

Life isn't fair. However, if you look at the bigger picture and embrace the concept of reincarnation, you'll see that divine justice fits perfectly into a higher plan.

We live in a dynamic world that is constantly changing; a dance of opposites seeking equilibrium. The wheel of life turns throughout the confines of linear time, bringing cosmic justice into your life. Existence is a continuous experience that is not limited to one incarnation. Some habit patterns in our present life may be an effort to balance actions initiated in past lifetimes.

I've found that people who have misused their power, failed to learn a spiritual lesson, or engaged in immoral activities in other lives find themselves driven by a compelling need to take action in their present life that will balance that behavior. This unexplainable need to overcompensate in this life is a *scale balancer*.

When Christine came to see me for a regression, she didn't have a particular problem to heal. She had just read a book on the subject of reincarnation and was curious to see what she'd discover. She was a full-time mom who worked part-time and definitely needed to relax.

Christine moved easily into the regressed state to a lifetime that was totally different from her present life. She knew that it was during the Renaissance and that she was a wealthy young Italian girl, with many admirers. I asked Christine how she spent most of her time.

"I'm dressed in a brocade evening gown, standing beneath a crystal chandelier in a large ballroom. I'm sipping champagne and talking to a few handsome young men. It seems like all I do is go to parties!"

I asked Christine to scan that entire life, while she was still in trance.

"I die rather young of some kind of disease. Although I socialized a lot, I never had any deep relationships. I was kind of shallow. I wasn't committed to anyone or anything, really. Even though it was entertaining, I felt kind of empty."

Christine then released the empty feeling by visualizing raindrops falling into a barrel. When the barrel was filled with cool, clean water, she began to laugh. She was overcome with a sense of happiness.

When Christine came out of the regression, she said, "Wow, I was so frivolous! I was just a party girl. I didn't need to work or do anything but have fun. It's the opposite of this life."

Christine realized that she was overcompensating in this lifetime by being overly responsible. Every day seemed to be a series of endless tasks. Yet she had already paid her karmic debt. She learned how to be responsible and have meaningful relationships. I recommended that she take a zinnia flower essence to help her to reclaim the ability to be lighthearted and playful.

It was such a relief to be able to relax that she booked a few more healing sessions. Christine realized that she worked constantly, with no time off to decompress. Over the course of a month, she changed her life by enrolling in a book club and a wine-tasting course.

Retrieve Scale Balancer Issues Exercise

Begin the karmic healing process by taking the first step, retrieving. To identify any past-life actions that may be emerging as out-of-balance action in your present lifetime, answer the following questions:

- What area of your life is out of balance?
- Does one area of your life get most of your attention and energy, at the expense of your well-being?
- In which areas of life are you lacking commitment?
- Do you frequently take on the role of rescuer or need to be rescued?
- Is there an area of your life in which you have no control?
- Do you feel you have to overachieve to prove that you are good enough?
- In what areas of your life are you struggling? Relationships? Money? Self-expression? Health?

Scale Balancer Meditation

If you feel you are leading an imbalanced life, this meditation will help you find out how to balance it. You may want to tape-record the script. You'll need the deck of tarot cards that you used in chapter 1. Go through the deck and find the Justice card, number eleven in the Rider-Waite deck. Sit upright in a chair with your spine straight, and place the card in front of you.

State your intention for this meditation. What do you want to know? It could be something like, "I want more information on how to _____."

Now turn on your tape recorder and play the meditation.

Focus on the card. Take in the whole image—the colors, the figure holding a sword in one hand and scales in the other. Close your eyes and see if you can recall the card in your mind's eye. Practice this until you can recall the card in detail if you are clairvoyant. Or, you may just have a sense of the card if you are clairsentient.

With your eyes closed, imagine the card growing larger and larger, until the figure in it is life-size. Step into the card. Look around you. What time of day is it? Are you indoors or outdoors? Get a sense of your environment. Do you hear any sounds?

Approach the tarot figure. She has a message for you. She can tell you the best way to balance the scales. Receive this message now. Let it flow into your mind. What do you need to do to be true to yourself? What do you need to do to be responsible for your actions? Take some time to receive any other insight. Watch the scales come to perfect equilibrium.

Thank the tarot figure and walk away. Step out of the card. When you do it, shrinks back into its normal size.

When you are ready, slowly open your eyes and come back into the room.

Answer these questions in your journal:

- What time of day was it?
- What type of environment was it?
- What was the weather like?
- Did you hear any sounds?
- What message did you receive?
- How are you to balance the scales?
- What do you need to do to be true to yourself?
- What do you need to do to be responsible for your actions?

Scale Balancer Affirmations

Synthesize the messages and guidance you've received in the meditation into an affirmation. Select from the list on the next page or make up your own affirmation to reprogram your way of thinking and bring balance into your life.

- I use my power wisely for the highest good of all.
- My life is filled with ease and enjoyment.
- I am good enough.
- I now have enough time, energy, and money to accomplish my goals.
- I receive all the love and support that I need.
- I honor my limitations and know what I cannot do.

Also, try sleeping with the Justice card under your pillow for a month as you undergo changes.

Scale Balancer Flower Essences

Use your affirmations in conjunction with one or more of the following flower essences to release negative ways of acting and imprint new positive images into your mind:

- **Rock water:** releases rigid, self-denying standards for oneself
- **Hornbeam:** releases the sense of being intimidated by everyday tasks
- **Elm:** lightens feelings of being overburdened or overextended
- **Larch:** releases the fear of making mistakes
- **Red chestnut:** releases the habit of being overly responsible for others
- **Fairy lantern:** releases immature and irresponsible behavior
- **Zinnia:** releases workaholic tendencies and the inability to play

State your affirmation each time you take your flower essence. Take two drops of the essence, four times a day. Continue to use the same affirmation and flower essence for at least a month.

More Resources

Repeating sacred Sanskrit words, or mantras, 108 times (about ten minutes) a day for forty days can bring about positive changes and healing. Mantras can soften life's hard lessons, attract abundance, and create healing.

You can find many beautiful recordings of mantras on CDs, including the following:

- *Healing Mantras* by Thomas Ashley
- *Jiva Mukti* by Nada Shakti & Bruce Becvar
- *Om Namaha Shivaya* by Robert Gass and On Wings of Song
- *The Essence* by Deva Premal

Summary

Now you've learned how karmic patterns have been influencing your body, emotions, thoughts, and actions. If you have taken the time to complete the exercises, you should be feeling like a brand-new you. Mail the second copy of your commitment letter to yourself now for continued support and encouragement. Schedule a coaching call with your support team.

In the next chapter, we will look at your first karmic relationships. We will explore your biological karma and ties with your ancestry and family members.

Part II

karmic ties with others

Chapter Five

Your Karmic Foundation

In part one of this book, you learned the tools of karmic healing. You healed unresolved soul issues and transformed karmic patterns. In part two, you will investigate karmic ties with your ancestors and family members.

In this chapter, you will look at your biological karma. You will discover what you've inherited from your ancestors and how that legacy impacts your life. The exercises will show you how to uncover the gifts and acknowledge the wisdom you've gained from life's challenges. You'll also learn how to draw power from your heritage and heal painful family circumstances.

Karmic Intermission

Have you ever wondered what will happen to your soul when you die? During a past-life regression, you observe significant moments of a past life. At the conclusion of a past-life regression, you are guided to view the cause of your death in that life and the type of funeral that was performed. You are directed to leave the body you inhabited in that past life to enter the exquisite realm of spirit, where there is no physical pain.

While under hypnosis, people who experience their soul as separate from their body feel euphoric. They are overcome with a deep sense of peace and comfort. They feel as if they are floating. Many past-life therapists call the post-death section of the regression the *interlife* phase. In this nonphysical dimension that is between incarnations, you receive healing by transforming any guilt, pain, and negativity you've been harboring into love and acceptance.

In the interlife stage, you have total access to your soul's wisdom. Therefore, you can view your past and present life with keen objectivity and clarity. Scanning your past life reveals more significant details and insights into the spiritual lessons you have learned. In this expanded state of awareness, you also receive guidance as to actions you need to take in your current life. After experiencing the interlife, people feel a deeper sense of purpose.

Past-life regression therapists agree that when your life is over, your soul goes to the spiritual dimension that you access during the interlife. Upon death, you stay in that spiritual dimension until you are reborn into a new incarnation.

Researchers have collected evidence that backs up the theory of the soul's immortality. Books such as *Remembering Your Life before Birth* by Michael and Marie Gabriel and Michael Newton's *Journey of Souls* focus on what happens to the soul between lives. In his book *Life after Life*, Dr. Raymond Moody recounts the near-death experiences of many people who were pronounced medically dead. The book includes many examples of people who recall leaving their bodies to arrive in a spiritual dimension where they experienced a sense of peace and freedom. Many survivors reported receiving assistance from loving helpers or spirit guides. Others recalled encountering relatives who have been deceased for years.

The time spent between lives is akin to being in a rest station, where you chart your next earthly journey. You decide what karma to balance and what lessons to learn. While you are in spirit, the knowledge you have accumulated from all your lifetimes is accessible to you. You can see your various weaknesses and strengths. You are able to plan the experiences that you need in your next incarnation to continue your spiritual growth.

Your Karmic Costume

The first karmic relationships people have are with their parents. You chose your parents by making a spiritual contract with them in the interlife. You might say "I was an accident; my parents didn't plan my birth." On a conscious level they may not have planned on having you, but on a spiritual level they agreed to do so. On a soul level you make choices all the time, whether you are aware of them or not.

Your biological karma consists of the physical, emotional, and mental patterns that you inherit from your mother's and father's ancestry. That karma has been passed down from generation to generation. Your biological karma is your *karmic costume*.

Have you ever wondered why you look a certain way? Or wish you had a different body? Imagine how different life would be if your skin were a different color. Your biological karma's purpose is to establish your identity as a member of a particular family and race. These physical patterns are encoded in your genetic makeup.

Your emotional and mental patterns are expressed through inherited prejudices, national rivalries, political views, religious beliefs, and so on.

On a personal level, your karmic costume will determine which foods, climate, and places you love or hate. Your biological karma may also be expressed in the form of addictions, alcoholism, or other compulsive behaviors.

You are probably very aware of some of your biological karmic patterns. For example, you may have an ear for music like your mother, a nose for business like your grandfather, a temper like your father, or the gift of gab like Aunt Betty. Do you have a particular talent that runs in the family?

If you're a woman, looking like your mother may not have any karmic significance, unless she resembles Marilyn Monroe or some other beauty queen. Physical beauty is a karmic gift and an asset. Similarly, being the spitting image of your dad may not mean anything special, if you are a male, unless, of course, he is six foot four and your dream is to become a football star.

Legacies, both positive and negative, are passed from generation to generation. What you inherit manifests on three levels. On the emotional level, your autopilot may have a combination of your parents' emotional responses. For instance, one time while stuck in a traffic jam, I noticed that I was becoming irritated and grumpy. I started to get impatient and was about to start obnoxiously blowing my horn when suddenly I remembered that I had a choice in how to behave. My emotional autopilot response was to act angry and frustrated like my father always did in the car, even though I hadn't driven with him in over thirty years.

On the physical level, you may suffer some of the same ailments as your forebears. If heart disease runs in your family, you could develop that condition unless you make a conscious effort to eat well, exercise, and reduce stress in your life.

On a mental level, you will have acquired your outlook on life from your parents. Your family members may be active in the same political party. Many families carry on a trade, with successive family members becoming carpenters, plumbers, mechanics, lawyers, or even actors.

You are also indoctrinated into your parents' religious faith, which gives you a moral code to follow. By the time you are an adult, you have integrated this code into your autopilot as part of your ethics, which you may agree with, rebel against, or modify to suit your own life.

In addition, you inherit your family's social status. Your economic class impacts your education, professional, and even marital opportunities. The beliefs passed down from your ancestors also contribute to your success, or lack of it.

These physical, emotional, and mental components you've inherited from your family make up your spiritual foundation, and you build your life upon this base. The more that you can accept what you've inherited from your family, both the curses and the blessings, the more successful you can be. If you feel estranged from your roots, now is the time to reclaim them.

Joy discovered that her karmic costume was a great gift. It seemed that her ancestors lived long lives. She inherited an earthy quality, which included a love for healthy food, for the sensuality of her body, and for the simple pleasures of life. These qualities were an asset to her becoming an outstanding yoga teacher.

Your Karmic Costume Exercise

Now it's your turn to find out why you chose your current karmic costume. This exercise can help you detect qualities that were passed down from your family so you can make the most of what you have. Write down everything you know about your heritage. Include the positive qualities as well as the negative traits. Get a deeper look at your biological karma by answering the following questions:

- In what ways do you feel in harmony with your background?

- In what ways do you feel disconnected from it?
- What are you learning by being part of your ethnic group?
- How does your ethnic heritage support your goals?
- How does your appearance benefit you?
- If you are lacking physical beauty, how does that impact you?
- What hardships do you face by being part of your ethnic group?
- What prejudices have you encountered as a result of your ethnicity?
- What fears or prejudices do you need to release?
- How has your family's social status impacted you? How has it influenced your level of financial success?
- What have you learned about expressing love and affection that you would like to release?
- What have you learned about expressing anger that you would like to release?
- How has your mother affected your beliefs about sex? Money? Career? Religion?
- How has your father affected your beliefs about sex? Money? Career? Religion?
- How has your brother/sister affected your beliefs about sex? Money? Career? Religion?
- What emotional patterns have you inherited that you'd like to change? That you'd like to embrace?
- What health patterns have you inherited that you'd like to transform? That you'd like to embrace?
- What thought patterns have you inherited that you'd like to release? That you'd like to embrace?
- What would you like to challenge about your family's teachings—overt and covert?
- How has your religious upbringing impacted your life?

Your Karmic Costume Meditation

Here's a meditation to help you gain power from your karmic heritage. First you'll need to collect photographs of your ancestors. Make photocopies of them so you don't damage your originals. Paste them onto a large sheet of paper or on an empty page in your journal. Paste them onto a family tree, if you know it, or just collage them together in a way that is pleasing to you. Are there animals, birds, or symbols associated with your group? If so, add the pictures to your collage. If your family has a crest or coat of arms, add those too. You can add special names or words.

Your fingerprints don't change throughout life. They mark your unique identity. Ink your fingerprints and stamp them onto your collage. Use whatever colors are pleasing to you. This represents the lifeline connecting you to your family tree.

Go to your sacred space. You'll do this meditation lying down. Place your collage at the crown of your head. Lie on your back and close your eyes. You may want to record the following meditation. Have your recording of the relaxation exercise (from chapter 1) available also. Take about thirty minutes to complete the meditation.

Breathe deeply and allow yourself to melt into a feeling of peace. Do the total body relaxation exercise. Allow your conscious mind to drift and dream and float off.

Imagine it's a beautiful summer day. You are in a peaceful meadow. The sun is shining and birds are singing. You come upon a path that leads deep into a forest. You set out upon that path, for you know it will lead you to a family gathering. You walk deeper and deeper into the forest. Colorful wildflowers line the path. Take note of your surroundings. Do you see any birds or animals?

You hear music, laughter, and sounds of merriment in the distance as you approach this gathering. These are your people. As you reach the group, a certain figure steps forward to welcome

you. What does he or she look like? What is he or she wearing? You may or may not recognize this ancestor. Note any thoughts, feelings, or body sensations you're experiencing.

The ancestor has a gift for you. Receive it now. What is it? Trust your impressions. How are you to use it?

The ancestor has something to show you. What is being revealed?

The ancestor has a message for you. Receive it now. Let it flow into your mind.

If you have a question, take a moment to ask your ancestor. Let the response flow into your mind.

Give thanks. Know that you can call upon your ancestral guide any time.

Take some time to explore any feelings, thoughts, or body sensations that may arise. What special qualities do the people at the gathering have?

When you are ready, say good-bye. Walk down the path through the forest to its edge.

When you reach the meadow, slowly open your eyes and return to the present.

Write down any impressions or guidance that you received. Draw any images or colors that may have been present.

Your Family Benefits

Incarnating into your family brings certain advantages. For example, everyone in my family loved to dance. My parents met at the Aragon Ballroom, where they went each weekend to listen to big bands and to waltz and do the rumba, fox-trot, and cha-cha. Mom and Dad always watched musicals on television, and they played a variety of albums on the stereo. There was music and dancing at all the holiday parties, and I would do the jitterbug, two-step, and twist.

Growing up in that environment helped free my self-expression. I love to dance. I have never been shy about expressing myself through movement, and I have taught belly dancing, performed, and worked with a modern dance company. Dance has been the backbone of my life. It has served me physically, emotionally, mentally, and spiritually. It has brought my community of students and audience members and myself much joy and satisfaction.

Family Benefits Exercise

Title a clean page in your journal "Positive Qualities." Take a moment to reflect on the benefits you received from your family. Make a list of at least five. Then answer the following questions:

- What qualities did you develop as a result of each benefit?
- What natural talents did your home environment encourage?
- How did these positive traits help you develop?
- How do they support you in achieving your goals?
- Thank spirit for these blessings.

Karmic Costumes and Past Lives

Exploring past lives can help you understand why you chose your current karmic costume and help you heal the unresolved issues attached to it, as in the case of my client, Aimee.

As a poet and a highly sensitive woman, Aimee always felt at odds with her father's heritage. His family came from Scotland in the eighteenth century and lived in New England. Relatives on that side of her family seemed puritanical, emotionally reserved, and not very self-expressive. Aimee was so different that she felt like an outsider. It was hard for her to relate to members of her own family. She came to my office because she thought a past-life regression could help her understand why she never seemed to fit in.

Aimee was eager to discover some answers, and she drifted easily into a deep state of relaxation. When she went into trance, she saw big hands coming out of a rawhide coat. She knew that she was a man named Charles and that he lived in Massachusetts.

"I am holding an old-fashioned musket in one hand and a dead rabbit in the other. There's a plain clapboard house in the snow. A woman is hauling wood inside. It's my wife. Yet I don't have any feelings for her."

I asked Aimee to recall an important incident in that life.

"I see a dinner plate piled with stewed rabbit placed on the table. My wife is sitting across from me. She is like a stranger. It's so quiet. There is nothing to say."

Aimee felt a deep sense of sadness and despair and began to cry. She released the grief and the painful memories that felt lodged in her throat by imagining balloons flying up into the sky. When Aimee came out of the trance, she felt lighter.

"Wow, who was I? How could I have lived like Charles? It was like a prison sentence."

It was a revelation to Aimee to discover a past life as someone totally opposite from who she is now. She loves her present life, giving live multimedia performances and expressing her feelings through poetry. She associates with musicians and other creative people and has had many passionate love affairs.

Realizing that she is living out a scale balancer, Aimee saw that she couldn't accept the traits of her father's family members because they reminded her of the emptiness of her past life as Charles. I suggested that she take a sweet pea flower essence to help her reclaim her roots and to affirm her heritage.

Aimee called me a few months later to say that she had had a major shift in relating to her relatives. She no longer judges them for being reserved, but accepts and loves them for who they are. As a bonus, she realized she had inherited the positive qualities of being hard-working and self-reliant. These qualities helped her be successful in her career. Aimee no longer feels like an outsider, and she is proud to be part of her family.

Mnemosyne—Remembering Meditation

The ancient Greeks worshipped a goddess of memory named Mnemosyne. She inspired the following meditation, which will help you to recall your soul purpose in choosing your current family. You will also explore the karmic ties between your family members and find out why have you come to the earth at this time

You may want to record the meditation on tape so you can practice and master it. Speak slowly and softly and pause after each sentence. Take about forty-five minutes for the entire meditation.

Go to the sacred space you have created. If it's night, turn down the lights. If it's daytime, pull down the shades. Light a candle or burn some incense to invoke a peaceful atmosphere. Play some soft music to set a quiet mood. You may want to take four drops of Desert Alchemy's flower essence Unsealing the Akashic Records Formula.

Before you begin the meditation, make sure you'll be comfortable. Stretch out in a comfortable position on the couch, on the floor, or on a bed. It's good to support your lower back by placing a pillow underneath your knees while lying on your back. Make sure you'll be warm enough. Your body temperature will lower when you go into meditation, and there's a tendency to get cold. Cover yourself with a wrap or blanket. Play the recording.

Close your eyes and take a deep breath. Feel your breath move through your body like a gentle wave. When you inhale, inhale peace. Exhale and let go of any tension. Inhale, breathe in relaxation. Exhale, let go a little more. Continue breathing deeply for a minute or two.

Allow all your thoughts to float away like feathery clouds in a baby blue sky. Feel a sense of lightness, a sense of peace, a sense of oneness. Enjoy this delicious feeling of relaxation. Visualize being encased in a protective cocoon of white light.

Imagine yourself in a playground on a beautiful summer day. The sun is shining, warming your skin. Feeling thirsty, you go to the fountain where a cool stream of clear water is flowing. You stop to take a drink. The water tastes sweet and refreshing. With each sip you feel happier and lighter. The weariness of the world slips away with each swallow, and you are filled with a sense of joy. All your problems seem to melt away.

With innocence and wonder, you take time to delight in the gymnasium there that is installed for your pleasure. You allow your inner child to come forth.

You forget to be so serious, for it's much more fun to be playful. There are swings, a sandbox, and a tunneled sliding board. You don't care about looking foolish. You are filled with a curiosity to try each one.

You take time to delight in the wonderful sensations each plaything has to offer. First you swing high in the air, enjoying the rhythm going back and forth, swaying back and forth, back and forth. Swinging into the clouds . . . feeling free and light.

After a while, you stop and run off to the sandbox. You sit in the warm sand and run your fingers through the silky grains. You find yourself burying parts of your body.

Then you gaily run off to the tunneled sliding board and begin climbing the ladder. Feel your foot on the first rung as you ascend, climbing higher and higher. As you hold the rail with each hand, it seems much higher than you thought. You climb still higher, feeling each foot climbing higher and higher until you reach the top.

You feel high in the air but secure, holding on to the railings with each hand. Each foot is securely planted on the platform, and you carefully sit down. You stare down into the tunnel, down into the darkness, preparing yourself for the ride down. You adjust your body.

When you are ready, you push off down the slide feet first and let go. Sliding faster and faster, you pick up speed, accelerating faster and faster. In the darkness the tunnel seems to go on for miles, sliding down, down, down.

At last you can begin to see a light getting brighter and brighter . . . You begin to slow down, gently coming to the end of the tunnel. Feet first, you step into the outside.

You are in a beautiful space, with trees, flowers, and a small stream of water in front of you.

A lovely woman with long hair wearing a white, flowing gown approaches you. Her smile makes you feel welcome, and a sense of peace fills your entire being. She holds a golden goblet in her right hand. She extends it out to you and beckons you to drink. You accept and raise the cup to your lips. As the red liquid inside the cup touches your tongue, you taste sweet nectar. You become filled with a sense of bliss, as if this were a potion made for the gods. The woman takes hold of your arm and walks you to the stream.

The water is as still and clear as a mirror. Gaze into the water and remember . . .

Why have you come to the earth at this time? Let the water reflect your soul awareness. Allow the answers to bubble up out of the water and flow into your mind. Trust your impressions.

Why have you chosen your family? Who in your family have you known before? Gaze into the clear pool.

Open your heart to remembering. Recall your prior relationship with the family member you knew before. Recall it in a way that is easy and comfortable. Let the images and thoughts come into your awareness.

What body sensations do you have? Do you feel any pain? Locate the pain or sensation in your body. Ascribe an image to it. How big is it? How much does it weigh? What kind of material is it made of? What color is it? How do you want to get rid of it?

Release the sensation of pain now into the white light of universal love.

The water seems so cool and inviting that you wade into it. It feels so refreshing that you lie back and float. The gentle current carries you away, light and free. It washes away the past, cleansing every part of you. Light, free, and weightless.

You'll remember all of what you experienced.

The water carries you ashore. Walking out of the water, you feel refreshed and energized, and up ahead you see the playground. You walk over to the playground, feeling good.

Walk over to the water fountain and drink. With each swallow, you begin to remember your present life.

Begin to feel your body, the space around you.

Count from one up to five. On the count of five, you'll be wide awake, totally refreshed, feeling good.

One, two, three, four, five . . . open your eyes and return to the present.

Take as much time as you need to write down any impressions, feelings, words of guidance, or body sensations that you experienced. Then answer the following questions:

- Why have you come to the earth at this time?
- Why have you chosen your present family?
- Who in your family have you known before?

- If you experienced pain or body sensations, what form did it take?

Karmic Costume Affirmations

Select one of the following affirmations or make up your own to reinforce your karmic costume healing:

- I am proud to be part of my family.
- My family loves and appreciates me.
- I am wanted and loved.
- I receive all the love and support that I need.
- I love and accept all of my family members.
- I am true to myself.

Karmic Costume Flower Essences

Try working with one of the following flower essences to help release negative karmic costume patterns:

- **Violet:** releases feelings of being an outsider
- **Sweet Pea:** releases the feeling of not belonging to your family
- **Willow:** releases the habit of blaming others for adverse situations
- **Centaury:** releases the need to be a people pleaser
- **Elm:** heals the inner child if you took on adult responsibilities of a dysfunctional family as a child
- **Pink yarrow:** releases oversensitivity in family situations

If you are feeling blocked, take an ancestral patterns flower essence, such as the one from Desert Alchemy (www.desert-alchemy.com), to recognize and integrate patterns inherited from your family.

Follow-Up Resources

For more ways to gain power from your karmic costume, consider doing one or more of the following:

- Study genealogy and research your family tree.
- Study heraldry and research your family's coat of arms, crests, totems, or other emblems.
- Research your family's surname.
- Cook traditional family recipes.
- Get a palm reading.
- Study phonology to determine the energy patterns in your name.

Karmic Cloaks

Your karma may involve missing family members. Perhaps you were adopted. Or maybe your parents divorced, died, or abandoned you. These types of challenging circumstances force you to develop in a particular way. While experiencing these painful circumstances, it's very hard to see that anything positive is to be gained from them.

I call this type of karmic situation, with its potential for growth concealed, a *karmic cloak*. There is power in accepting the fact that you are the source of your experience and that you attract the lessons that you need to learn. In this model there is no blame, only acceptance of responsibility.

During a workshop, I asked participants to write down their family members' names as part of a karmic costume exercise. Maria, a middle-aged housewife, raised her hand.

She shared her story with the group, with an anger and bitterness in her voice. "I don't have a father. He left before I was born."

I asked where she was born.

"Calabria, in southern Italy," she replied.

Thinking that Calabria is one of the most gorgeous places on earth, with its rugged mountains and ancient ruins looming against the crystal waters of the Mediterranean Sea, I said, "Oh, how beautiful."

She disagreed, "No, it was horrible."

When I asked her to look underneath her karmic cloak to discover the spiritual lesson she snapped, "There wasn't one."

I gently coaxed her to keep looking. A moment later, her chest heaved and tears trickled down her face. She put her face in her hands and started to weep.

She murmured, "It was so hard; we were so poor."

After releasing the grief she'd been carrying for all those years, she was able to recognize and own her karmic cloak. Looking back, she saw that her karmic lesson was to learn independence and self-reliance. She had fulfilled her dream of immigrating to America and had a good, comfortable life. It had taken much strength and determination to do it.

Her eyes welled up with tears again as she exhaled a sigh of relief, and her face softened as she released her bitterness and felt a sense of peace. In that moment, she looked ten years younger.

Maria's karmic cloak was definitely related to this current lifetime, but it may also have been a life lesson carried over from one or even several past lives. She doesn't need to explore the past life she may be balancing. She got the lesson! And that's what matters.

Karmic Cloaks with Existing Family Members

Karmic cloaks also can appear as a break in a relationship with a parent, as in Elise's case. She is in her fifties and the mother of three grown children.

Elise came to see me for a reading because she was having difficulty dealing with her mother. Her mother was in her eighties, blind in one eye, and diabetic. For the past four years, her mother had had her own apartment in an assisted living community.

Being with her mother was painful for Elise, for it seemed there was nothing Elise could do to please her. When Elise would arrive at her mother's apartment, her mother's typical welcoming remarks would be, "You've gained weight. What an awful outfit you have on. Your hair looks terrible."

Between the nasty remarks, they would sit together in a strained silence. Elise dreaded every visit, but she felt obliged to go. She was considering not visiting her mother anymore.

I intuitively felt that Elise was harboring some hurt from the past, so I asked her to look within and describe how she felt about her mother. She was surprised to discover that she was carrying resentment from when she was a teenager. I listened patiently as she told her story.

"Throughout high school, I was groomed to go to college. My dream was to be a teacher. But when I graduated, my mother said there was no money, so I couldn't go. Feeling I had no alternative, I eloped with a man my mother didn't approve of. From then on, our relationship began to deteriorate. She began to criticize me and call me stupid. It's been like this for the past thirty-five years."

I applied the karmic healing principles of responsibility, recognition, reason, and forgiveness and asked, "Your kids are grown and have married. Do you want to go back to school?"

She said, "No, not really. But I saw to it that all of my children had college educations."

At that moment, Elise saw that she had chosen the karmic path of being a mother. She realized that she could have worked her way through college, but didn't choose to do so. She now claimed responsibility for her actions.

I then asked Elise if she could release the anger she'd been holding since she was eighteen years old. Eagerly, she visualized her anger, which was in her stomach, as a boulder. She then imagined it blowing up and turning it into thousands of sparkles.

I asked Elise, "If people are in your life for a purpose, how does relating to your mother help you grow?"

"I'm never nasty to my children. Being negative is like giving out poison," Elise replied.

I asked Elise if she could forgive her mother. She said, "Oh, yes; she was even right about my husband."

She laughed and felt lighter and free. Before leaving my office, Elise promised that she'd visit her mother on Sunday.

Elise called me on Monday to tell me what happened.

"On Sunday, as I was driving to visit my mother, I felt scared and some resistance. But I knew this was in God's hands. When I arrived, the first thing Mom said to me was, 'You're wearing Grandmother's pin. It's so pretty.' She then took out her jewelry box and gave me four beautiful brooches. I can't remember the last time she gave me anything. We then went shopping and had a great afternoon together. No nasty words were spoken. We hugged and made plans to get together for the holidays. Driving in the car, I cried with happiness all the way home."

When Elise released her pent-up anger from the past and stopped blaming her mother for her own karmic choices, her mother was able to relate to her in a better way. When you do your inner work, the people in your life will respond as if they have taken a self-improvement workshop too. When you are being great, it creates the space for others to be great as well.

Healing Karmic Cloaks Exercise

If you were adopted, abused, or a victim of incest, undergoing therapy is the best way to deal with rage, grief, and feelings of abandonment. If you have completed therapy, this next exercise can help you heal on a spiritual level.

Answer the following questions in your journal to help you see how you grew and developed from experiencing a karmic cloak:

- Did you have a karmic cloak situation at birth or shortly after?
- If a parent was absent, how did that impact you? What was the hardship? How did you triumph in the situation? How did the experience force you to grow? How did the experience help you develop spiritually?
- What lesson did the karmic cloak conceal?
- Did a karmic cloak situation happen later in your life?
- How did it force you to grow?
- What did you learn from it?
- Can you let go of it now?
- Can you apply the karmic healing principles of responsibility, recognition, reason, and forgiveness to this experience?

Hanging on to resentment and bitterness will block you from living fully in the present. It is difficult to confront the painful emotions of the past, but once you release them, you open a door for more happiness and contentment to enter. You'll be able to feel more self-love, and in doing so, you'll be able to receive more love from others.

Healing Karmic Cloaks Meditation

When you have forgiven the parent(s) who left or hurt you, you will be free from those karmic chains. This visualization can help you to forgive and forget.

Go to your sacred space. Relax into a comfortable position and close your eyes. Breathe deeply and allow yourself to melt into a feeling of peace.

Imagine that you are relaxing on your favorite beach on a beautiful summer day. A gentle breeze caresses your skin. The sand feels warm and inviting under your bare feet. You take a moment to dig a hole in the sand at the water's edge. The tide is slowly coming in.

Now imagine your parent who abandoned or hurt you. Feel the grief or anger as it bubbles up into your awareness.

Now visualize the grief leaving you and going into the hole you dug. Let go of the hurt. Let go of any sensations in your body relating to the hurt. Keep sending those sensations into the hole. Let go of any feelings of being unlovable. Let go of the loneliness. Send those feelings into the hole.

When you have released it all, see the tide come and fill the hole. Your pain is totally dissolved into the water.

Say out loud with sincere intent, "I forgive you."

When you are ready, run into the water. Feel the sea's healing energy cleansing you. Play in the water as long as you wish. When you are ready, come back onto the beach.

You feel refreshed, renewed. You feel physically lighter.

When you are ready, slowly open your eyes and come back into the room.

Write down anything you experienced in your journal.

Karmic Cloak Affirmations

Select one of the following affirmations or make up your own to help heal your karmic cloak.

- I forgive my father.
- I forgive my mother.
- I am wanted and loved.
- I forgive myself for all the times I have abandoned someone else.

- I give myself permission to be totally satisfied.
- I release all my suffering, and I let in the light of healing grace.

Karmic Cloak Affirmations

Flower essences to help heal issues of abandonment include the following:

- **Baby blue eyes:** releases a feeling of rejection by one's father
- **Evening primrose:** releases a feeling of rejection by one's mother
- **Mariposa lily:** releases a feeling of abandonment due to lack of bonding with one's mother and supports the ability to be nurtured
- **Holly:** releases a feeling of being unloved
- **Sweet chestnut:** releases a feeling of abandonment by God

Summary

By now, you should have a renewed sense of honor and gratitude for your family. Since you have vital information on why you selected your present family, your relationships can take on a deeper meaning. You've discovered how your hardships have shaped your character and have brought you jewels of wisdom. You've learned how to access power from your ancestors and strengthen your foundation. With the help of flower essences and affirmations, you feel a greater sense of belonging, love, and inner peace.

In the next chapter, we'll look at the karmic ties among individual family relationships and how to transform them.

Chapter Six

Healing Family Relationships

In the last chapter you learned that your biological karma sets the foundation for your life. Your family relationships provide your primary spiritual lessons, for they give you the opportunity to reap the consequences of your past actions and transcend them.

In this chapter, we'll take a look at the role individual family members play in your life. You'll see how easy, loving relationships affirm your highest qualities, while difficult relationships can motivate you to grow. The exercises will help you learn how to bring harmony to relationships that clash. You'll also learn how to restore and rejuvenate your energy if you're dealing with a challenging relationship.

Cosmic Role-Play

When one person harms another, it's usually because of ignorance or some form of negative cultural conditioning. The perpetrator may be completely unaware of the other person's pain or suffering. However, there is no escaping the law of karma: what you give out comes back to you. You may discover in a past-life regression that the root of a present-day relationship problem stems from a time when you were irresponsible, and thereby harmed another. By switching roles in your present life, you experience the pain you previously inflicted.

Adriana did a series of past-life regressions. She wanted to gain some insight into her family, the most important part of her life. In the first regression, she saw herself as a man in Poland who succumbed to a gypsy dancer's charms and left his family behind in order to be with the woman. His wife had no means of support and was forced to give up her son for adoption. Brokenhearted and destitute, the wife died of pneumonia a year later.

In another regression, Adriana was a peasant woman in France. Her husband died in a boating accident, leaving her grief-stricken and alone to raise their child.

In a third regression, she saw herself as Paolo, a young boy in Italy. Paolo's father was seduced by the neighborhood seamstress and left the family to become the woman's paramour. Paolo was devastated. Adriana completed this karmic circle by experiencing abandonment as a child.

After that lifetime, her experience was complete. By switching roles throughout different lives, Adriana had balanced the karma resulting from her initial abandonment of a wife and child. In her present lifetime, her twenty-eight-year marriage has resulted in two healthy children, and she is passionately committed to her devoted husband.

Karma plays out in your relationships. Your soul picks a family who will collaborate with you to balance your karma and learn your lessons. You are drawn to people that you have bonded with during previous lives. These ties may include indebtedness, or they may simply be based on love. Whatever the case, these relationships ensure that everyone has the potential to benefit by being given an opportunity to grow in some way.

Karmic Family Relationships

You may share past-life histories with your parents, siblings, or other family members. The roles may be distinctly different in various lifetimes. For instance, your mother may have been your daughter in a prior life. Your brother could have been your uncle, or your sister could have been your teacher. Sometimes you don't share a past-life history with your family members. However, you are magnetized by people who behave as you once did in another life. You are drawn to such people because of the law of attraction: like attracts like.

Here is a brief description of the karmic relationships played out in family situations:

- **Karmic catalysts:** Relationships that present painful lessons that force you to grow. Like being in a karmic boot camp, you are trained to become stronger.
- **Karmic coaches:** Especially close relationships that help you through a crisis and/or affirm your positive attributes.
- **Karmic clinkers:** People who illustrate a negative quality in you, which motivates you to grow in the opposite way.
- **Karmic clashes:** Interactions with people who have very different beliefs from yours and expand your vision of the world.

Karmic Catalysts

A karmic catalyst is a challenging relationship that forces you to make great sacrifices or wounds you in some way. The hardships that it brings compel you to be strong and to toughen up. Kirsten is Toby's karmic catalyst.

Every time Toby visited my office, she burst into tears as soon as she sat down. When her daughter, Kirsten, failed first grade, teachers suggested that a psychologist should evaluate her.

Kirsten was diagnosed as having a learning disability. Toby was getting divorced at the time of the diagnosis.

Now a single parent, Toby moved to a small town so Kirsten could go to a school that would accommodate her special needs. Kirsten isn't like other children. She has a communication disorder, so she can't always say what she means. It could be ninety degrees in the car, but instead of saying, "Put on the air conditioner," Kirsten may say, "Turn on the heat." She can't distinguish breakfast from dinner or Tuesday from Saturday. She can't grasp the concept "I'll be back in five minutes."

Even though Kirsten looks normal, with her blond hair and pretty blue eyes, she has poor motor control. She can't do what ordinary children do, like ride a bicycle or roller-skate. Other children find it hard to relate to her. Other kids don't understand why Kirsten mixes up her words or can't return a ball in a simple game of catch, so she doesn't get invited to birthday parties or overnight sleepovers.

When I asked Toby how Kirsten's disability impacted her life, she wept.

"It's hard. I've had to put my life on hold to raise her by myself. I wish I could be a normal parent. I always feel like the odd man out. Some mothers talk about getting their daughter's cheerleading outfits. Others brag about their child making the science team. I was excited when Kirsten finally learned to write her name in third grade."

As Toby drifted into the trance of a regression, she felt that her feet had deep holes or wells in them, as if she had no toes. I asked her whether she was crippled.

"No, I don't experience myself as crippled."

Toby began to sob as she released the negative energy from her aura by imagining her feet being filled with light. I asked her to listen to her inner guidance for a message.

"Kirsten doesn't see herself as disabled. She wants me to see *her*, apart from her handicap," Toby exclaimed.

At the end of Toby's session, I asked her how having Kirsten for a daughter made her grow. She replied, "It's so easy to dismiss someone because they are unlike everybody else. I see how important it is to validate people, even if they are different. Everyone has a contribution to make. Everyone's voice counts."

Karmic Catalyst Lessons

Another type of karmic catalyst can take your psyche on a one-way ride to hell. With this type, you'll spend a good deal of your time crying or cursing while you are tested to see whether you will make it or break. Eddy was Maureen's karmic catalyst.

Maureen had reached the end of her rope in dealing with her grown son, Eddy. Eddy got involved with drugs, lost his job, and was plummeting into a downward spiral. He was addicted to Oxy-Contin but refused to go into a rehab center. In fact, he wouldn't accept any help because he wouldn't admit he had a problem. Maureen found it difficult to sleep at night, since she was plagued with worry. She'd arrive at work feeling tired, stressed, and distraught. Recognizing that she needed support while dealing with her son, she began a series of healing sessions with me.

When I pointed out that Eddy made his own choices, Maureen stopped blaming herself for failing as a mother. When she realized that Eddy was choosing his particular drama for his own spiritual growth, she began to heal. Over a few months, she came to terms with the fact that Eddy might not straighten out. Clearly that would be his choice. Maureen's final ordeal came when Eddy died of a drug overdose before his twenty-ninth birthday.

In addition to receiving many healing sessions to help her cope with her loss, Maureen took a borage flower essence to uplift her spirit and give her courage to face the future.

When Maureen examined the spiritual lessons presented in her relationship with Eddy, she saw that she hadn't thought she had the strength to endure his death. But in surviving, she discovered an core of spiritual fortitude that she didn't know she had.

Karmic Catalyst Exercise

If you have had a karmic catalyst relationship, answering the following questions can help you to rejuvenate:

- Are you related to a person who is a karmic catalyst?
- What is the hardship? How are you triumphing in the situation? How does the experience force you to grow? How is the experience helping you to develop spiritually?
- What hidden lesson are you learning?

When you have forgiven the karmic catalyst and forgiven yourself, you will be free from those karmic chains.

Rebirth Rituals

Many people who have had karmic catalyst relationships experience a psychological transformation. They pass through the dark night of the soul to experience a rebirth. Here are three rebirth rituals to restore your energy and rejuvenate you.

It's best to perform the rituals on the night of a new moon before bedtime. You'll need about twenty minutes for the bath, fifteen minutes for the restorative yoga pose, and five minutes for the tarot visualization.

RITUAL BATH

You'll need to gather the following items:

- A timer
- Candles: blue for healing, white for purification, and pink for love
- Incense (your favorite scent)

- Meditation music
- One cup of Epsom salt, sea salt, and baking soda, combined
- Essential oil: rose, sandalwood, or lavender
- A flower essence from the list below
- A white bathrobe (optional)

Now you're ready to cleanse in your ritual bath:

- Create a peaceful atmosphere in your bathroom by lighting candles, burning incense, and playing relaxing music.
- Fill your bathtub with hot water. Add the salts and baking soda, four drops of essential oil, and four drops of flower essence. (Pregnant women should avoid using essential oils and hot water.)
- When the tub is filled, you may want to enter your sacred space wearing a white bathrobe.
- Set your timer for twenty minutes.
- As you enter the bath, intend that the water heal, purify, and restore your spirit.
- Allow yourself to relax.
- You may want to imagine a butterfly breaking out of a cocoon. Imagine its colored wings emerging from their shelter. Experience the butterfly taking flight. See it soaring into the sky, light and free.
- When the timer chimes, imagine that you are being reborn as you step out of the saltwater, the amniotic fluid of mother earth. Just as the butterfly was reborn emerging from the cocoon, so are you reborn.

RESTORATIVE YOGA POSE

You'll need the following items:

- A timer
- An eye pillow
- Two blankets

Prepare to relax in the yoga pose called Viparita Karani, or Legs up the Wall:

- Clear a space in a room where you can lie comfortably on your back with your legs inverted and supported by a wall.
- Set your timer for fifteen minutes.
- Lie on your back and place a folded blanket beneath your sacrum. Scoot close to the wall, with your bottom snug against the wall and your legs stretched straight up the wall.
- Relax your legs against the wall.
- If you like, cover yourself with the second blanket so you stay comfortably warm.
- Place the eye pillow over your eyes.
- Place your arms at your side, palms up.
- As you exhale, feel your belly soften.
- As you inhale, imagine that you are melting into the floor.
- Feel your whole body relax into the earth.
- Allow yourself to rest deeply until you hear the timer.

REBIRTH TAROT VISUALIZATION

You'll need your Rider-Waite tarot cards. Take out the card that is labeled Strength. Sit upright in a chair, with your spine straight, and place the card on a table in front of you. Focus on the card. Take in the whole image—the colors, the figure, the lion, and the roses. Take in the power of this card—the strength, the fortitude. Tune into this card for about five minutes. You can repeat this meditation until you really feel the card's energy. You may want to tape it on your mirror or sleep with it under your pillow.

Before going to sleep, make a wish for something you want to happen. Write it down. Sleep with a rose quartz crystal either under your pillow or placed at your bedside table. You should awaken feeling a restored sense of well-being.

Karmic Catalyst Flower Essences

The following flower essences can help heal karmic catalysts:

- **Oak:** provides endurance during long struggles
- **Aspen:** helps you face the unknown courageously
- **Mountain pride:** helps you confront darkness and become a spiritual warrior
- **Baby blue eyes:** promotes faith in a spiritual destiny despite harsh experiences
- **Gentian:** develops perseverence despite setbacks
- **Honeysuckle:** helps life go on after a death or loss

Karmic Coaches

Not all karmic relationships are difficult. Occasionally, people feel an almost unnatural closeness to a particular relative with whom they relate easily with loving affection. This intense bonding is frequently based on shared past-life experiences, although recognition of this phenomenon is usually absent. These karmic coaches support you through difficult situations or crisis. They have character traits that affirm your own goodness. A karmic coach is clearly and almost always on your side.

Tamara was gorgeous. She was blessed with strawberry blond hair and a beautifully sculpted body. She worked as a runway model for local fashion shows with her daughter, Kate, another natural beauty.

When Kate was in her last semester of high school, Tamara left the house for a doctor's appointment. It was one of those perfect spring days. The sun was ablaze, tinting everything with a soft golden glow. Dogwoods and tulips abounded. Children frolicked on their bikes, and all was right with the world.

Tamara hummed to herself as she waited at a red light in her Camaro. When the light turned green, Tamara failed to look to her left as she drove into the intersection and thus missed seeing the black Cherokee running the light. The other car crashed into the driver's side of Tamara's car. Semiconscious, she was rushed to the hospital.

A concussion was the least of her problems. Her ribs were fractured, and she had lost most of her teeth when her jaw was nearly broken. When Tamara awoke in her hospital room and looked into a mirror, she was horrified. She felt like a millionaire who had lost everything in the 1929 stock market crash. All she wanted was the courage to jump out the window. As she saw it, all her beauty and health were gone.

Weak and dispirited, Tamara felt like she was dying. While her pain was excruciating, her mental anguish was even worse.

"I'm not human," Tamara thought as she caught a glimpse of herself in the mirror.

Throughout the numerous operations and reconstructive surgeries that followed, Tamara's husband maintained a grueling work and travel schedule, leaving him little time to show his support. Fortunately, Kate became Tamara's karmic coach. Oftentimes, Tamara was so depressed that she didn't want to get out of bed or speak to anyone. While Tamara lay in bed convalescing, Kate devoted herself to her mother's recovery. With nary a complaint, she cooked dinner, did the laundry, swept the floors, bathed Tamara, and kept a cheery attitude.

"Mom, you'll get through this. Everything is going to be fine. You'll get better."

Years later, when Tamara and Kate attended my healing classes, I learned that they had opened a spa together. As you would expect, their skills were synergetic. Kate had numerous certifications in healing arts and was enrolled in nursing school. Tamara was a specialist in skin care and permanent makeup. Tamara looked and felt absolutely wonderful.

"I'm a survivor," she affirmed. "But I simply could not have made it without Kate."

You don't have to experience a situation as dramatic as Tamara's to discover your karmic coaches. The following exercise is designed to help you understand the karmic lessons your family relationships are teaching you.

Karmic Coaches Exercise

List the names of all your family members. Include people with whom you've been out of communication or who have died. The list could include parents, grandparents, siblings, children, spouse (or former spouse), aunts, uncles, cousins, nieces, and nephews. Now answer the following questions:

- Who are your karmic coaches? Who are the people who are/were supportive?
- Whom do you relate to very easily?
- What are their strengths or qualities that you admire?
- How have they impacted your life?
- Which family members inspired you to be a better person? How did they inspire you?
- How have your family members brought out the best in you?

Take the list of positive qualities you've just gathered and set it in front of you. Go to your sacred space and reflect on those qualities. Allow your imagination to create a past-life character based on those characteristics. Write a one-paragraph scenario of a person who embodies these admirable traits. Even if you think you can't write, allow your imagination to flow.

Resist editing or rewriting it.

What insights do you have about yourself after completing this exercise?

Does the story relate to a particular area of your life or an issue with which you have been struggling? If so, what is it?

You may prefer to make a collage instead of or in addition to your story. Go through magazines and tear out images that resonate with the positive qualities you've listed. Glue them in your journal in a way that is pleasing to you. Try not to think about it too much. Don't worry about trying to make it perfect.

What have you learned from your story? What does it tell you about yourself through its images and symbols?

Karmic Coaches Flower Essences
The following flower essences can help to affirm positive qualities:

- **Buttercup:** increases self-worth
- **Larch:** promotes confidence in your creative abilities
- **Mallow:** develops confidence in social situations
- **Trumpet vine:** promotes vital speaking and self-expression
- **Tansy:** contacts your true source of energy
- **Mullein:** helps you fulfill your potential

Karmic Clinkers

On the other hand, have you ever noticed any character traits of close relatives that were so repulsive that you vowed never to be like them? Have you ever said, "I *never, ever, ever* want to be like . . . ?" These people are karmic clinkers.

Karmic clinkers can be narrow-minded, or they may have bad habits that annoy you. You may not have shared a past life, but their karmic purpose now is to help you upgrade your personality. They show you a negative quality that you most likely had in a past life. They will help you understand the impact of your past actions and motivate you to keep growing in the opposite way.

Both of my parents were karmic clinkers. My mother was very fearful, to the point that she wouldn't go anywhere by herself. She was too afraid to take a bus and too scared to learn to drive. She always had to rely on someone else for her source of transportation. I just couldn't comprehend her fear. It seemed so unreasonable that I vowed to be independent. Since taking that vow, I have traveled around the world by myself.

My father had his first heart attack when I was five years old. It was very traumatic for me because I was my daddy's little girl. He had high blood pressure, smoked like the proverbial chimney, never exercised, and basically ate meat and potatoes and *more* meat and potatoes. He refused to change his health habits even though his physical condition consistently deteriorated, and he spent a great deal of time in and out of the hospital before dying in his late fifties.

Watching my father suffer had a deep impact on me. I did not want to wind up like him. Observing his condition motivated me to take responsibility for my own health. In my teenage years, I realized that what I had been eating had no relationship to what my body really needed. After years of consuming greasy hamburgers, even greasier fries, and Coke, my taste buds were shot. Not to mention that I was chubby, not my favorite body type.

I simplified my diet, became a vegetarian, enrolled in dance classes, and joined a gym. In a matter of months, I was more energetic, as the accumulated toxins realized that my body would no longer be a friendly host.

Upon reflection, my parents gave me great gifts. Watching my dad reap the consequences of his bad habits gave me the incentive to take control of my health. Ultimately my new path led me to study herbology, yoga, dance, and various forms of holistic healing. Mom showed me that if I let fear run my life, I wouldn't see much of the world.

Karmic Clinker Exercise

List the names of at least ten important people in your life. Include people with whom you've been out of communication or who have died. The list could include parents, grandparents, siblings, children, spouse (or former spouse), aunts, uncles, cousins, nieces, and nephews. Answer the following questions:

- Who are your karmic clinkers? Who has traits or habits that are unacceptable to you?
- What do they do that grates on your nerves?
- How do their actions inspire you to be a better person?

Take the list of negative qualities you've just gathered and set it in front of you. Go to your sacred space and reflect on those qualities. Allow your imagination to create a past-life character based on these negative traits. Write a one-paragraph scenario of a person who embodies them. Even if you think you can't write, allow your imagination to flow. Resist editing or rewriting it.

What insights do you have about yourself after completing the exercise? Does the story relate to a particular area of your life or an issue with which you have been struggling? If so, what is it?

You may prefer to make a collage instead of or in addition to your story. Go through magazines and tear out images that resonate with the negative qualities you've listed. Glue them in your journal in a way that is pleasing to you. Try not to think about it too much. Don't worry about trying to make it perfect.

What have you learned from your collage? What does it tell you about yourself through its images, colors, and symbols?

Karmic Clinker Flower Essences

Use Desert Alchemy's Remembering and Releasing flower essence formula to cleanse general unwanted patterns inherited from your family. Also, use the following:

- **Walnut:** releases unwanted habit patterns inherited from others
- **Sunflower:** heals self-image internalized from father
- **Fairy lantern:** releases patterns of emotional immaturity due to an overprotective mother
- **Yarrow:** protects from absorbing negative thoughts and feelings of others

Karmic Clashes

Another type of relationship is the karmic clash. These clashes involve interacting with people who shake up your belief systems and expand your worldview. They help you to break out of old ways of thinking and being. Karmic clashes usually occur between family members because you probably wouldn't befriend people whose values, beliefs, and tastes are the polar opposite of yours, or even downright scary.

Georgia had a hard time accepting that her daughter, Robin, was gay. And it blew her mind when Robin brought home the love of her life. When Sylvia, a six-foot-tall, broad-shouldered transsexual with pink dreadlocks, a glittering nose ring, and a lamé miniskirt sat down for Thanksgiving dinner, it was beyond anything Georgia had ever imagined.

When I pointed out to Georgia that she was having a karmic clash with Sylvia, she realized that she had very rigid, traditional values around love and sex. She understood that just because her beliefs were right for her, it didn't mean they were right for Robin.

Georgia's relationship with Robin and Sylvia expanded her worldview to accept that people do things differently. It took a while, but they now really enjoy being together as a family. Sylvia even turned out to be a great cook!

It was crucial to Donald that he present an impeccable public image in his small town. He lived in a pristine, Beaver Cleaver house on Main Street, with a white picket fence and with pink petunias blooming in the front yard. He was an usher at the Episcopal church on Sundays and a member of the Jaycees. However, he was also known to crack racist jokes at the country club. When his blond-haired, blue-eyed daughter announced that she was pregnant and the African-American star of her high school basketball team was the father, Donald was unable to accept this karmic clash. Although his daughter was looking forward to having an interracial marriage, Donald couldn't cope with the situation. The stress it brought on was too great. He died of a stroke two weeks prior to the wedding.

Mia experienced a karmic clash when her husband of seven years announced that he had a secret life as a cross-dresser. She was shocked to find boxes and boxes stored in the attic containing high heels, wigs, make up, negligees, and lace panties.

During her past-life regression, Mia uncovered a life in which she was a highly judgmental priest who condemned many people who dared to enjoy sex. She related it to her current life, for she had a strict religious upbringing with rigid views of sex. Even though she eventually got divorced, Mia credits her husband in shattering those rigid ideas about sex and gender. Her view of life expanded and she is more accepting of those who are different.

Karmic Clash Exercise

List the names of your family members. Include people with whom you've been out of communication or who have died. The list could include parents, grandparents, siblings, children, spouse (or former spouse), aunts, uncles, cousins, nieces, and nephews. Answer the following questions:

- With whom do you have karmic clashes? Is there someone who thinks so differently from you that you have trouble relating to them without getting into an argument?

- What do they believe that shocks or upsets you?
- How do you benefit from seeing another point of view?
- When you can't accept another person's point of view, how do you react? How does that reaction diminish the love you give and receive?

Karmic Clash Hint

If you are stuck on being right about your point of view, you may be one of the following:

- Dogmatic
- Self-righteous
- Judgmental
- Condescending
- Pompous
- Zealous
- Opinionated
- Close-minded
- Dictatorial

When you are fixated on expressing one of the above negative qualities, you usually experience a breakdown in communication. Love doesn't thrive under these conditions. When you can accept the other person and their point of view, you will be free from those karmic chains.

Karmic Clash Visualization

You can work through karmic clashes by using the following visualization:

- Close your eyes and relax.
- Visualize your karmic clash in a pink bubble of light.
- Affirm that you give the freedom to be who they are.

- Give yourself permission to think differently from the person with whom you have a karmic clash.
- Affirm that you have perfect communication.

Karmic Clash Flower Essences

Try working with one of the following flower essences to improve your relationships:

- **Vervain:** releases the need to convert others to your beliefs
- **Vine:** releases the tyrannical disregard for the autonomy of others
- **Water violet:** releases seeing oneself as better or higher than others
- **Yellow star tulip:** promotes an awareness of what others are feeling
- **Calendula:** develops tolerance for what others are saying

Summary

When healing your biological karma, you discovered that painful relationships with family members have served a purpose: they've challenged you to become stronger. You now have tools to renew and rejuvenate yourself. It's probably easier now to appreciate relatives who are very different from you. You've acknowledged the good qualities you've developed and affirmed your attributes, so you are feeling very positive.

In the next chapter, we'll explore relationships outside the family—with friends and co-workers. You'll learn how to complete and heal unsettled scores. Mail the third copy of your commitment letter to yourself to give you continued support, or schedule a coaching call.

Part III

Healing Karmic Unions

Chapter Seven

Healing Karmic Relationships

In part two of this book, you explored your karmic ties with your ancestors and family. In part three, you will investigate karmic relationships with bosses, lovers, and those with whom you need to heal.

Sometimes meeting a person can trigger intense unexplainable emotions, which arise unexpectedly, just as visiting a place or watching a movie can bring about a feeling of déjà vu. When we are ready to spiritually heal, we attract certain people that cause unsettled scores to surface. In this chapter, you'll learn how to detect and resolve these relationship issues through writing exercises and a releasing ritual. You'll also learn how to heal painful relationships from the past and how to attract your perfect partner.

Karmic Awakenings

Did you ever meet someone and feel like you had known him or her for a long time? Maybe you were so in tune with each other that you finished each other's sentences. Perhaps you knew when the telephone rang that it was that person. You were so connected, but you couldn't explain it.

On the other hand, did you ever meet someone and intuitively know that the person was going to be trouble? You had a bad feeling about the person, but you couldn't pinpoint what the problem was? Certain relationships can trigger unresolved soul issues.

Love and hate are two powerful forces that act like karmic glue, connecting your destiny with others throughout lifetimes. Love ties you to your friends, family, and loved ones, and you are joyously reunited time and time again. Unresolved issues involving hate, rage, anger, and revenge tie you to others as well.

Your soul knows what you need to accomplish. In the interlife you make contracts not only with your family but also with others who aren't blood related so that your soul will continue to develop. Contracts with friends, co-workers, and lovers are designed to teach your soul lessons that promote your spiritual growth.

If we keep repeating the same mistakes lifetime after lifetime, we get stuck in the same predictable behavior patterns and limiting beliefs, and we become stagnant. If we keep missing our lessons, eventually our soul will say, "Enough already!" When we're in-between lives in the interlife, sometimes we plan a dramatic situation to wake us from our spiritual slumber.

Spiritual awakenings can happen through a circumstance or in a personal relationship. Sometimes an incident involves a deep loss and is shocking enough to shake us out of our personalities. Life-shaking calamities demand our complete attention so we have no choice but to listen to our higher selves.

For example, Lydia came into my office because she was emotionally distraught. She was shocked to discover that her husband was having an affair with his co-worker. But to make matters worse, he was fired from his job because it was against company policy to have personal relationships within the office.

The incident was devastating for Lydia, so she requested a healing. In her session, by practicing the principles of karmic healing, she looked within herself to see what role she played in the situation. She discovered that communication had broken down in her marriage. She loved her husband, but they had stopped sharing their intimate feelings and had grown apart. Lydia saw that this calamity happened for a reason. It was an opportunity for healing and growth. She also realized she had it in her heart to forgive him.

What appeared to be a catastrophe brought about a transformation, the catalyst Lydia and her husband needed to get in touch with what was really important. They began talking to each other again and went to see a marriage counselor. In the process, they renewed their vows to each other. Her husband found another job and they relocated to another part of the country to start a new life together. Their relationship is more satisfying than ever.

Karmic Carryover

Awakenings frequently come through relationships. The most unlikely people can be catalysts for change. If you are in a relationship that is causing you stress, the problem could be rooted in a past life. There could be a karmic reason for you having to deal with a person who is very negative. If someone harms you and is not forgiven, the anger and hurt is carried into another life. I call an unsettled score from a past life a karmic carryover.

Unresolved soul issues stay in your aura and form a karmic clog. When you are ready to heal, your karmic clock kicks in the circumstances that trigger a crisis, so the stuck energy can be released. Sometimes the person with whom you have an unsettled score will appear in your life. When your karmic carryover is released or balanced, you usually go your separate ways. You are free to move on to your next challenge, as Carrie did.

Carrie found her ideal job as a sales rep for an art gallery. Who wouldn't love being surrounded by beautiful paintings and having a prestigious clientele? Plus she received a commission from all she sold. So why was she a nervous wreck? Since beginning her position nine months earlier, she had taken up smoking and gained ten pounds.

The source of her stress was her boss, Karl. He was always undermining her. When a potential buyer would walk in the gallery, Carrie would begin her sales pitch. A half hour later, after enrolling her customer into buying a particular work of art, Karl would burst out of his office with his charismatic smile and shoo Carrie away. Karl would close the deal, and Carrie wouldn't receive a commission. This happened over and over.

Carrie was fed up. Karl had left for his two-month summer vacation and would be unreachable at his beach house in South Hampton. The day after he left, Carrie discovered that the business account was empty. There was no money left to pay her salary or the artists whose paintings had been sold months before. Apparently, Karl had used the money to renovate his summer home and left her at the gallery high and dry. Business was very slow in the summer months. If she didn't generate a sale, there would be no income.

Carrie was so distraught that she came to see me for a psychic reading. I suggested that she try a past-life regression to help her relax and gain insight into her situation. As she drifted into a trance state, she looked down to see that she had a large man's hands with thick fingers. On her right hand she wore a gold ring with a huge sparkling diamond. Then, when she looked at her legs, she discovered she was wearing man's trousers and brown loafers. The man was walking down the hall of a huge office building to meet someone.

Carrie's heart began to pound as the shadowy figure in the hall came into focus. "It's Karl . . . He's my business partner."

Carrie felt enraged and clenched her fists. Her face turned bright red, and drops of perspiration beaded up on her forehead.

"He cheated me out of my share of the money! I hate him!"

She realized that she had died shortly afterward, drowning in a boating accident. She never forgave Karl for his shady financial dealings.

"Are you ready to forgive him now and let go of this?" I asked.

"Yes." She visualized her fury as a raging fire. She released it from her aura by imagining rain falling onto it. When the rain stopped, she visualized a gentle wind blowing all the ashes away.

While still in trance, Carrie laughed, "He's still the same fast-talking shyster."

At the end of her session, Carrie felt much better. Her body felt light, and she could breathe freely again. She vowed to quit smoking and handed her pack of cigarettes over to me.

The past-life regression helped Carrie to see Karl more clearly. Karl always thought of himself first, and he undermined anyone who got in his way. She had been taking his actions personally because of the anger she held toward him.

After Carrie had completed her karmic work with Karl, her life changed very quickly.

The next day, she made two sales that covered the gallery's business expenses for the summer. She and the artists would get paid, and she'd even receive her commission.

One week later she serendipitously ran into her high school sweetheart. She hadn't seen him in years. They rekindled their relationship and two months later they eloped. When Karl returned in the fall, she quit her job. The last I heard, she had moved and went back to college.

Karmic Carryover to Balance the Scales

Sometimes your actions in past lives create a karmic carryover for someone else. You will attract the person and circumstance to balance the scales. You will encounter someone who behaves inappropriately, just like you once did, in order to see how inappropriate behavior impacts others.

You may have unknowingly encountered a karmic carryover and asked yourself, "What was that all about?" Or "What was his/her problem?" From a karmic healing perspective, the question to ask is, "What is the lesson for me?" Here's a tip. If you are forced to deal with a person whose behavior is irrational, confusing, and challenging, it's probably a karmic carryover.

Most people don't consciously know why they seek out a past-life regression. Usually my clients say they are just interested. Timothy didn't have a burning issue when he came into my office to explore a past life. He said he was simply curious as to who he may have been. However, through the regression, he got in touch with a relationship he hadn't thought about for years.

When Timothy connected to his past life, he saw that his hands were brown and wrinkled. He was a Buddhist monk wearing a dark red robe, holding a staff, standing on a stone walkway in the mountains of Tibet. He felt tired but very peaceful.

He knew that he traveled to different villages to perform ceremonies and healings, as well as to mediate and counsel. The country was on the brink of war. The Chinese had attacked several villages, and the monks were there to keep peace.

I asked Timothy to experience an important incident in that life. Tears gently trickled down his face as he remembered.

"There is a fire; everything is burning. I see a meditation hut; a special place where we would go to be alone is in flames. Oh my! This sacred place is burning . . . it's gone!"

He sobbed as he recalled, "An elder, a most holy person, died in the fire. The monks had so much anger. We lost control and nearly killed the arsonist. It was shameful. Our actions were the opposite of what we preached. We were tested and we failed."

I asked Timothy if he recognized anyone there from his present life.

"Oh my God! The man who started the fire was William, my ex-boss!"

I then guided Timothy to visualize William in a pink bubble of light and release any negativity related to William. Timothy imagined all his rage and grief releasing from his aura by visualizing a flock of birds soaring high in the sky. "I forgive you, William," Timothy whispered.

When Timothy came out, he felt a deep sense of peace.

"I haven't thought of my ex-boss in ten years. This explains a lot! Working with him at the newspaper was a struggle. The man's temper tantrums were so unprofessional; I found it hard to deal with him. He was always trying to provoke a fight, but I never responded. I was tested over and over, but I never succumbed to violence. I guess I passed!"

Karmic Carryover Issues Exercise

There are two ways to heal a karmic carryover. One is to forgive, the other is to ask for forgiveness. This exercise will help to create forgiveness and a sense of closure.

Begin by taking responsibility for the part you play in challenging relationships. Examine how you are behaving in the relationship. How do you contribute to the conflicts? Ask yourself the following questions:

- Are you forced to deal with someone who is negative, inconsiderate, or irresponsible?
- Do you have unrealistic expectations?

- Do you put up with unacceptable, inappropriate, or abusive behavior?
- Do you allow another person to act with low integrity (not keep his or her agreements)?
- Are you unable to ask for what you need?
- Do you constantly feel angry and resentful while in certain relationships?
- Do you make childish demands?
- Do you find yourself always mishearing or misinterpreting other people?
- Do you frequently get into arguments?

Forgiveness Exercise

This exercise will also help to heal a karmic carryover by creating forgiveness. Go to your sacred space and write a letter to the person you want to forgive. You can begin your letter by saying something like, "I'm sorry for how our relationship turned out. Please forgive me for being _____." You can state how angry and hurt you were. Say everything. Bare your soul. Cry, weep, and be angry. Get it all out.

See if you can place yourself in the other person's role. Try to understand why he or she acted the way they did. Remember the good times. Acknowledge how you both grew emotionally or spiritually when you were together. How did you prosper? At the end of the letter, thank the person for the contribution he or she has made to your life. Wish them a blessing, if you can.

If it is appropriate, mail the letter. If not, either shred the letter or burn it in your fireplace.

Forgiveness Visualization

Go into a state of deep relaxation. Imagine a pink bubble of light surrounding the person you want to forgive. If your visual psychic sense is developed, you may actually see the person in the bubble. If you can't visualize, paste a photograph of the person inside a circle cut out of pink paper.

Talk to the person. Have a one-way imaginary conversation with the person. Talk it all out, the good times and the bad. At the end of the conversation, thank the person for the contribution he or she has made to your life. Wish them a blessing, if you can. When you are finished, release the pink bubble into the white light of universal love. Shred the photograph and pink paper bubble, or burn it in your fireplace.

Karmic Carryover Flower Essences

Here are some flower essences you might try to help you forgive and forget:

- **Beech:** promotes forgiveness of others' faults
- **Pine:** helps one forgive oneself for one's own errors and mistakes
- **Sage:** encourages making peace with life
- **Heather:** helps you to understand the suffering of another
- **Yellow star tulip:** develops empathy
- **Pink monkeyflower:** helps you to retain trust and vulnerability despite previous heartbreak

Karmic Revenge

If you feel as though you've been cheated, used, or manipulated, the natural impulse is to be vindictive. We're programmed for survival and retribution. Our mass media supports this base, primal point of view, with violent images dominating television and movies.

The audience cheers as Clint Eastwood tracks down the villains and kills them. The popular *Godfather* stories are about mobsters who take the law into their own hands and get even with those who hurt their family members.

I'm not encouraging you to be a victim. If you've been assaulted or abused, call the police and take legal action. Don't try to settle the score on your own. Give your case to the proper authorities and let the law of karma balance the scales.

If you've been betrayed or rejected, the instinctive response is to strike back. However, taking revenge doesn't solve the problem, it just perpetuates unresolved karma, begets more negativity, and often escalates a conflict. Besides, engaging in negativity wastes energy you could be using to create something positive.

Revenge can trap you in a vicious cycle. If you are walking around feeling angry and resentful, you are probably alienating others. Instead of forming loving relationships, you are actually keeping people away by creating a barrier around yourself. When you push people away, you are left alone with your anger and resentment. You end up feeling powerless, blaming others for your predicament.

Karmic Revenge Awareness Exercise

To determine whether you are motivated by feelings of revenge, ask yourself the following questions:

- Is there someone who has betrayed you whom you haven't forgiven?
- Is there someone who has cheated or deceived you whom you haven't forgiven?
- Are you hanging on to hurt that happened years ago?
- Are you still angry with someone whom you haven't seen in years?
- Do you harbor thoughts of revenge?
- Are you blaming someone else for your problems?

Releasing Ritual

Hating someone is like shooting yourself and expecting the other person to be wounded. You are the one experiencing the toxic feelings. So if you were planning to sneak into your ex's apartment to add a depilatory to the shampoo bottle, stop and take a breath. Try a releasing ceremony instead.

This ritual can help you release a relationship that ended badly. Give yourself plenty of time to perform the ceremony and then some down time to process the emotions that will be transmuted. You may need to sleep more. It's best not to schedule social obligations for a few days while you are integrating and healing.

For this exercise you'll need:

- A gift for mother earth, such as tobacco, cornmeal, candy, or a coin
- A small thin stick or twig about six inches long
- A small stone about the size of a quarter
- A knife or scissors to cut the string
- Two magic markers: black to represent feelings for revenge, and violet to represent forgiveness and peace
- A piece of string about twelve inches long

Find a place outside that feels comforting and nurturing where you can have privacy. Give a gift to mother earth in exchange for the stick and stone. You can offer some tobacco, a pinch of cornmeal, a piece of candy, or a coin.

- Color the stick black. Color the stone violet.
- Relax into a comfortable sitting position and close your eyes.
- Breathe deeply and allow yourself to feel centered and calm.
- Express your intent to your higher self to be free of this person. Ask yourself if you are willing to let go. If your inner response is yes, proceed; if no, try the ritual at a later date

- State your intent to release the person. Ask that this healing be done for the highest good of all.

- Hold the black stick and recall the betrayal or the incident that caused the breakup. Recall your body posture, what you said, what you heard, what you did. Where are you holding the emotion in your body? Is it stuck in your throat or lodged in your belly? Do you hold it in your forehead or in your shoulders? Penetrate the feeling with your awareness. What thoughts are associated with this feeling? Break the black stick as you tell your inner self to release any trauma related to this incident. Let the thoughts go too. You may feel hot or waves of energy pulsing through your body. After you experience the sensations, you may begin to feel lighter. Some people experience a tingling sensation in their hands or feet. (You may need to repeat this and break the stick a few times.)

- Now pick up the string. Imagine that you are holding one end and that the person you are releasing is holding the other. Say out loud, "I release you," as you cut the string. Offer a good wish or a blessing. Know that you no longer hold this person, and they no longer have a hold on you. Allow any feelings of sadness to surface.

- When the sadness has disappeared, pick up the violet stone and hold it next to your heart. Tell yourself that you accept that releasing this person is for your highest good. The relationship has served its purpose. Know that the universe will provide you with more relationships. You will always attract the right people, at the right time, according to what your soul needs to learn. If you can, forgive the person. Forgive yourself. You both did the best you could. Recall some of the good times you shared. The love will be with you forever.

- As you hold the violet stone, allow feelings of peace and tranquility to fill your being. Affirm that all of your relationships are in divine order and they manifest with grace in perfect ways. You may feel tired.

Bury the stick and string, or burn them in your fireplace. Place your healing stone on your altar or in a special private place where it won't be disturbed for twenty-one days. After that, give the stone back to mother earth. Be very gentle with yourself during this healing cycle.

Karmic Revenge Flower Essences

Try working with one or more of the following flower essences to support the changes that you will undergo in the next three weeks:

- **Bleeding heart:** releases unhealthy attachments in relationships
- **Honeysuckle:** releases nostalgia for the past that blocks being in the present
- **Love lies bleeding:** releases intense pain and suffering
- **Pink monkeyflower:** releases feelings of rejection
- **Holly:** releases hatred and the desire for revenge
- **Willow:** releases resentment

Karmic Values

Many people in unsatisfying relationships don't have a clue as to what they really want. Often they choose unsuitable partners simply because they don't understand what is really important to them in a relationship. Many times, it is because they are on autopilot, living out patterns, learned in childhood, which no longer promote soul growth.

In Brittany's family, money equaled power and control. Gifts always came with strings attached. There was always an unspoken contract, "I'll give you money, but only if . . ."

During her counseling session, she became aware that she always attracts men who can't give freely. She saw that her time and affection are always up for sale. Brian, the man she recently had begun dating, offered to pay for her plane ticket to Paris. But her "free" trip had an unspoken price. She would be Brian's escort and bed partner even though they barely knew each other.

While the session was enlightening, Brittany wasn't ready to do the work she needed to do to break the pattern she was mired in. She never returned for a regression and snubbed my suggestion that she go into therapy. The last I heard, she was vacationing in Spain, staying as a "house guest" of her new love interest. Of course, each of us has a choice. This was hers. On another note, let's look at Marge.

Marge had just ended a relationship with Lonnie and wanted a past-life regression to help her resolve her feelings. She and Lonnie were so different, yet they were drawn together from the moment they met.

In the regressed state, Marge knew that she was in Chicago during the nineteen twenties and that Lonnie was her husband.

"I am wearing a white satin negligee, lounging on a red velvet couch in a large Victorian mansion. I am waiting for my husband to come home."

I asked her to move to the root of her problem with Lonnie. Marge burst into tears.

It's Lonnie. . . . He's been murdered. He was involved in business dealings with gangsters. A rival mobster gunned him down."

The session helped Marge release her grief and allowed her to understand her deep feelings for Lonnie. It also helped her resolve their differences in their present life. He was a powerful man involved in big business. He lived in a prestigious neighborhood and drove an expensive sports car. In contrast, Marge worked as a schoolteacher, lived in a historic home in a community-minded neighborhood, and drove a sedan. She realized that she felt uncomfortable at Lonnie's glamorous parties. Their values were poles apart. The past-life tie made them feel very comfortable together, but their goals in this life did not support a lasting relationship.

The regression helped her to let go of Lonnie and discover what was truly valuable to her. By her third session, Marge had started dating someone who was far better suited to her. The sessions helped her resolve her feelings quickly and enabled her to move on to new and healthier experiences.

Karmic Values Exercise

If you want to create a relationship, try using this simple exercise to get clear on what you truly want. Sending a clear message to the universe is the first step in making it happen. Open a blank page in your journal and answer the following questions:

- What are your values?
- What qualities do you strive to have in your life?
- What is important to you on the material level?
- How much money do you really need to earn to live comfortably?
- Do you love your job? Or do you work just for the money?
- What is important to you in a friendship?
- What qualities really matter to you in a relationship?
- Are you attracted to a pretty or handsome face? Or is a person's character more important?
- Does the size of a potential partner's bank account matter to you more than having good personality traits?

Attracting Love Visualization

Go to your sacred space. Have your journal with you, along with a collection of magazines and a pair of scissors to cut them up.

In your journal, list twenty-five qualities that are essential to what you'd consider a good partnership. Make sure you include that the person is available, the appropriate gender, and lives nearby. Qualities may include someone who is fun, understanding, reliable, resourceful, health-conscious, independent, thoughtful, romantic, nurturing, and so on.

Close your eyes and visualize your completed list surrounded in a pink bubble of light. Imagine sending it out into the universe, knowing that it will attract your perfect partner to you.

Now make a collage of images that represent the qualities you want in a partnership. Go through magazines and cut out pictures that reflect the kind of relationship you'd like to have. Paste them together on a fresh page in your journal.

You may want to tear out the page and hang the completed work in a prominent place in your house.

Karmic Values Affirmations

Select one of the following affirmations or make up your own to help attract love:

- I am attracting my ideal lover.
- There's an abundance of lovers who are perfect for me.
- I am open to receive love.
- I am highly attractive to men.
- I am highly attractive to women.
- I am loved for being myself.

Karmic Values Flower Essences

Try working with one of the following flower essences to help attract a romantic partner:

- **Basil:** integrates sexuality and spirituality in a love relationship
- **Hibiscus:** integrates love with passion
- **Larch:** releases feelings of being sexually inadequate
- **Sticky monkeyflower:** releases fear of intimacy
- **Calendula:** opens communication with others
- **Holly:** opens the heart to giving and receiving love

Summary

Now that you have done the forgiveness exercise, you have claimed a new life free from guilt and resentment. You are probably feeling a lot lighter and more peaceful. Since you have released unhealthy attachments, people may be responding to you with much more love and kindness. You've become clear about what is really important to you in a relationship, which is the first step in attracting a perfect partner.

In the next chapter, I'll give you the tools to heal karmic romantic relationships.

Chapter Eight

Healing Karmic Romantic Relationships

How can unresolved soul issues influence your romantic relationships? They can manifest in great or small power struggles—fighting over the toothpaste cap or over thousands of dollars. They can also appear as a lack of commitment or illicit affairs. In this chapter, you will learn four types of challenging karmic romantic contracts that have the potential to transform you. You'll also learn how to heal failed relationships and understand why your romantic life may be off kilter. The exercises will help you realize why you choose certain partners (even knowing that there will be trouble ahead), bring a new perspective to commitment, and gain a fresh look at the balance of power in your present relationship.

Karmic Relationships

Do you ever fantasize about meeting your soul mate? Perhaps you have a burning attraction for someone who is already married? Or maybe you're in a committed relationship, but you're considering cheating on your partner because you found someone who seems utterly irresistible? Have you ever met someone who you thought was Ms. or Mr. Right, but discovered that you couldn't live together after all? These types of attractions that are so intense they touch your soul are usually karmic.

In romantic relationships, when you have a soul connection with another person, you have an extraordinarily strong emotional tie as well. The bond can be so strong that you become overwhelmed by emotions you feel toward the other person. In these types of relationships, it's typical to act impulsively and to not use good judgment.

Karmic relationships can appear in the following ways:

- **Karmic red flags:** relationships in which hazardous conditions exist; exercise caution in these relationships for they are truly treacherous.
- **Karmic replays:** situations that you also experienced in a past life. The people's names may have changed, but it's the same setup. You didn't learn the first time, so here's another chance.
- **Karmic shadows:** relationships that help you get in touch with a part of yourself that has been kept in the dark. Whether a person or a situation, they help you see where you are not being responsible.
- **Karmic flip-flops:** relationships that are role reversals. Both of you are working to heal a previous life where there was unequal power in the relationship. As a result, one person suffered. Being placed in the other person's shoes helps you to balance the scales.

In the interlife, you contract with souls that you have known romantically throughout other lifetimes. These soul contracts are challenging and are designed to awaken you to your negative patterns of behavior or to strengthen your character. If any of these contracts are at play in your life, it means you are ready to release old ways of thinking and behaving that no longer serve you. Locating and distinguishing a negative pattern is the first step in transformation.

Karmic Red Flags

When it comes to relationships, people make some crazy choices. Over the years I've worked with people who have attracted destructive romantic partners. I call this type of a relationship a karmic red flag because hazardous conditions exist and there is a need to exercise caution. Something inside you knows that being intimate with the person isn't really in your best interest, yet you ignore the warning signs and get involved anyway. Usually the relationship quickly becomes an ordeal, your karmic alarm is triggered, and you wake up. Hopefully you wake up to a new level of awareness.

Bill Clinton is the perfect example of someone who had it all—marriage, family, and a powerful position of leadership—yet he risked losing it when he responded to a karmic red flag and had an illicit affair. Ultimately the crisis that he went through brought healing to his wounded inner child. He went into marriage counseling and for the first time examined how his childhood issues impacted his emotional life. His marriage was saved and is probably functioning in a better, healthier way.

You may have been born into a loving family and had an idyllic childhood. Yet as an adult, you may attract an inappropriate partner because your soul yearns for wisdom and healing. The difficult experiences generated by a karmic red flag pave the road to learning and growth. Emotional devastation can offer an opportunity to rebuild your psyche on fresh new ground. Your wounds can open you up to a new spiritual level that you might not have reached otherwise.

A karmic red flag usually creates a crisis situation in which you are driven to a breaking point, thus it is similar to a karmic cloak or a karmic catalyst. The relationship becomes a spiritual trial by fire, and you are given the chance to fly like a phoenix or be reduced to ashes.

Pamela's husband, Jason, was her karmic red flag. See if you can spot the warning signs.

When Pamela moved to New York City from a small town in the Midwest, she was anxious to be in a relationship. The minute she met Jason, they became so attached to each other that they couldn't bear to be apart. Six weeks later, when he proposed that they elope, she said yes. When Pamela called her family to announce that she had married in an impromptu ceremony at city hall, her parents sent a generous check as a wedding present.

Pamela quit her job to work for Jason's company and moved into his apartment on the Upper East Side, not knowing that his mother, Ellen, lived down the hall in her condominium. On their first night home after honeymooning in the Virgin Islands, the phone calls began.

"Jason, can you come over? My bedroom light has burned out. It's too high for me to reach. I need you to replace it," Ellen beckoned.

"Oh hello, Pamela. My refrigerator is empty; can I come over for dinner?"

"Jason, can you drive me home from work?"

One week later, they were no longer a happy couple. Pamela realized that she was part of a love triangle. She felt like she was a second wife in a polygamous marriage, her mother-in-law being wife number one. Daily life was a constant battle for her husband's attention. When Ellen called, Jason dutifully went running.

When Pamela received her monthly credit card statement, she was alarmed to find three thousand dollars' worth of unaccounted extra charges.

"Oh, those must be mother's charges. I put her on our charge account, in case she needed something. Don't worry; I'll take care of it," Jason said.

But he didn't take care of it. When Ellen's lavish spending maxed their credit card out, the couple decided to use some of their wedding gift money to pay off the debt rather than risk ruining their credit.

Jason's company began growing by leaps and bounds, as did Pamela's belly. She was pregnant. The intellectually stimulating conversations they had while courting were long gone. All they seemed to do now was argue.

"We need to move out of here. The baby is coming soon, and we need more room. We can use the rest of our wedding money for a down payment," Pamela stated as she picked up a real estate guide.

"We can't afford it just yet," Jason would argue.

While Pamela was in the last stages of pregnancy, Ellen was giving birth to her own scheme. Owning an apartment in New York wasn't enough to satisfy her; she wanted a beach house too.

When Pamela discovered that Jason had paid Ellen's entire beach house mortgage with the remaining wedding present money from her parents, she was so upset that she went into early labor. Eight hours later, she was the mother of a baby girl.

Being a mother gave her the strength to give Jason the final ultimatum.

"It's either me and the baby, or your mother! Choose!"

"Mother has sacrificed so much for me. She raised me alone after my father walked out. I can't leave her," he answered.

When Pamela phoned me for a reading, she was emotionally distraught. The first step was to apply the principles of karmic healing. She needed to take responsibility for the role she had been playing in her marriage. The session helped her realize that she had been too open and trusting. She was so eager to have a family that she had lost her judgment. It was naïve of her to marry Jason before she really knew him. Their strong karmic tie had clouded her thinking.

Pamela had allowed herself to be used, but not anymore. The next day she mustered up enough courage to file for a divorce. However, the ordeal wasn't over yet, for Jason and his mother wanted all of Pamela's money plus custody of her daughter.

The next five years were spent in grueling legal battles with Jason and Ellen. Over the course of that time, Pamela went through many changes. During many healing and counseling sessions, she examined how she needed to develop. She realized that she had inherited her naivety from her mother.

Pamela's mother lived a very sheltered life. She had no experience in dealing with people outside of the family and was as innocent as a fairy tale princess. She lived in a make-believe world, where everyone was loving, thoughtful, and considerate. Pamela realized that she too had this false idealism and lacked the ability to truly see a person's character. Pamela was now transforming that karmic pattern into wisdom. She no longer blindly trusts people.

During her dark, bleak days in court, Pamela grew stronger. I recommended that she take a sweet chestnut flower essence to bring her spiritual comfort.

Eventually she won custody. Most important, Pamela vowed that she would never try to control her daughter's life. She would never be selfish like Ellen.

Karmic Red Flag Issues Exercise

Karmic red flags compel you to look within and seek to understand yourself. To discover whether you have karmic red flag issues, ask yourself the following questions:

- Are you in a relationship that you know isn't good for you?
- Are you stuck in a love triangle?
- Do you have illicit or secret affairs?
- Do you trust someone who has proved to be untrust-worthy?
- Do you become intimate with someone before you really know him or her? If so, does that really work for you?
- Are you so afraid to get involved with someone that you avoid relationships?
- Are you addicted to love? Sex?
- If you have been involved with a karmic red flag, what did you tell yourself to avoid responding to the warning signs?
- What did you learn from the relationship?
- How did your character flaws play into the situation?
- Did you fail to assert yourself?
- Were you communicating openly and honestly?

Karmic Relationship Meditation

The following meditation is designed to give you insights into a past life that you've shared with a specific person and to understand the karma carried over from the relationship. You can use it to receive guidance for any relationship, not just a red flag.

You'll examine the purpose of your present relationship and get information on what you need to do to: learn to heal, balance the scales, and be complete.

You may want to record this meditation. Take plenty of time to pause after each question to allow enough time for the information to come through. Don't rush. The whole process should take about forty-five minutes. Have an intention to meet a specific person. Insert his or her name in all the blanks. You can rerecord this meditation to explore as many relationships as you like.

Relax into a comfortable position. Close your eyes and take a deep breath. Feel your breath move through your body like a gentle wave. When you inhale, inhale peace. Exhale, and let go of any tension. Inhale, breathe in relaxation. Exhale, let go a little more. Continue breathing deeply for a minute or two as you release all of your concerns of the day.

Begin to feel a sense of lightness, a sense of peace, a sense of oneness. Enjoy this delicious feeling of relaxation. Visualize being encased in a protective cocoon of white light.

Imagine that you are boarding an airplane. Your flight is scheduled to take you to a past life that you shared with _____ [insert the person's name].

You sink into your spacious, comfortable seat in first class. You fasten your seat belt and relax, finding safety within the core of your being.

Feel yourself moving through time and space, moving through time and space. Moving to another lifetime that you shared with _____ .

When the plane reaches its destination, you will be in the past life that you shared with _____ .

The airplane is descending now, descending into that past life. The plane smoothly touches the ground.

You've landed safely. You get up out of your seat and leave the airplane. As you walk through the door and step out of the aircraft, you step into another lifetime. Look down at your feet. Are you wearing shoes? Look down at your hands. Are you male or female? What color is your skin? What sensations are you feeling in your body? What kind of clothes are you wearing? About how old are you? What is your name?

Open yourself deeper into your intuition. Trust your impressions as they flow into your mind.

You walk up the long hall. At the end of the hall, _____

is waiting to greet you. You can see him or her standing in the shadows. As you approach closer and closer, his or her image becomes clear.

Is _____ male or female? What color is his or her skin? How old is he or she? What is he or she wearing? Experience the emotion of seeing or experiencing your loved one. Notice any body sensations. What are you thinking?

What is your relationship with this person? Just allow the answer to flow into your mind.

_____ takes your hand to show you to your home. Gently allow yourself to recall the memory, easily and effortlessly. Where are you? What country are you in? What is the year? Take some time to explore. Recall it in a way that is easy and pleasurable.

And now move to an important incident.

What are you experiencing? What are you feeling? What sensations do you feel in your body? What are you thinking? Are there words being said? Allow the story to unfold. Open to your inner guidance.

How does this experience resolve? What is the outcome?

Next, move to the time of your death. View it in a way that is easy and comfortable. Trust your intuition.

How did you die? Allow the impressions to surface from the deepest part of your memory.

Now scan that entire life. Allow the thoughts, insights, and wisdom from that life to surface into your awareness.

What was your spiritual lesson in that lifetime? What is the karmic connection between you and _____ ? Allow the wisest part of yourself to emerge. What is the purpose of your relationship with _____ in your present life?

What do you need to do to heal? What do you need to do to balance the karmic scales? What do you need to do to be complete?

What body sensations do you have? Do you feel any pain? Locate the pain or sensation in your body. Ascribe an image to it. How big is it? How much does it weigh? What kind of material is it made of? What color is it? How do you want to get rid of it?

Release it now into the white light of universal love. Fill your whole body with white light. Imagine this white light coming down your face, down your neck, down your torso. Feel this white light giving every cell of your body permission to function in perfect health. You are healing on all levels—physical, emotional, mental, and spiritual.

In just a few moments you will count from one up to five. On the count of five, you'll be wide awake, totally refreshed and feeling good.

One ... two ... three ... four ... five. Open your eyes and return to the present.

Give thanks for the insights you have received.

Take as much time as you need to write down any impressions, feelings, words of guidance, or body sensations you had. Use colored pens to draw shapes or images. Then answer the following questions:

- What were your impressions of your self in that past life?
- What were your impressions of _____ in that past life?
- What was your relationship?
- What country were you in?
- What was the year?
- What was the important incident?
- How did this experience resolve?
- How did you die?
- What emotions, body sensations, or thoughts did you have?
- What was your spiritual lesson in that lifetime?

- What is the connection between you and _____ karmically?
- What is the purpose of your relationship with _____ in your present life?
- What do you need to do to heal?
- If you experienced any pain or body sensations, draw an image of them.

Karmic Red Flag Affirmations

Select one of the following affirmations or make up your own to reinforce your karmic relationship healing:

- I forgive _____.
- I am becoming the right person.
- I do not need _____ to survive.
- I receive value from all of my relationships.
- I make good decisions.
- I trust myself.

Karmic Flower Red Flag Essences

Try working with one or more of these flower essences to support your healing process:

- **Sweet chestnut:** provides comfort when experiencing the dark night of the soul
- **Sunflower:** restores self-esteem
- **Borage:** provides courage to face an ordeal
- **Sagebrush:** helps to accept loss
- **Oak:** keeps one centered and strong in the face of adversity
- **Oregon grape:** helps to regain faith in people
- **Mountain pride:** provides courage to confront evil or wrongdoing

Karmic Replays

If you missed the boat and failed to learn a particular lesson in a past life, often you are offered a second chance. I call these rerun situations karmic replays. Your current life will parallel a situation you experienced in a past life. The circumstances may be quite different, yet the theme is the same. It's like Bill Murray in the film *Groundhog Day*. He relives the day over and over, trying different responses to the circumstances, until he discovers how to live well. The difference with a karmic replay is that you're repeating a life, as opposed to a day. If you are in a karmic replay, the relevant relationship is usually one of high drama or crisis to get your attention, as in Bobbi's case.

Bobbi often wondered about her past lives. After she completed one of my reiki healing courses, her life began to undergo many positive changes. Eager to keep growing, she scheduled a past-life regression. As she drifted into a deep trance, she recalled being a young woman named Emma in eighteenth-century England. She saw that she was reaching out to a man whom she knew was George, her current husband, though he looked totally different. Tears streamed down Emma's face as this young man told her that they couldn't be married.

"My father will not allow it," he said.

Bobbi continued to sob as she relived Emma's bitter pain and rejection. Emma died in her early thirties, never mending her broken heart.

As Bobbi came out of her trance, she looked calm and peaceful. She told me how the past life applied to her present.

"Oh my God, I can't believe it! I met George, my husband, twenty-five years ago at a car dealership. I was the office manager, and he worked in sales. It was love at first sight. Three months later, he moved into my house. When George told his family about our wedding plans, they threatened to disown him.

They hadn't even met me, yet disapproved because I was five years older than George, divorced, and not Catholic.

"George assured me that he still loved me. 'The money doesn't matter, honey. No one can stop us from getting married.'

"George and I went ahead with our wedding plans. Two weeks before the wedding, George's father called him with an ultimatum: 'If you marry Bobbi now, you will be disinherited. You will no longer have contact with anyone in the family. To us, you will be dead. If you wait one year and your love survives, we will accept her.'

"We cancelled the wedding. I knew that George would resent me one day if he lost contact with his family. The year passed quickly. I converted to Catholicism, and we were married in the Catholic Church. Over the years, I've been embraced and accepted by his family—even his father!

"Now I know why George and I went through such an ordeal. We were tested yet again. However, this time our love survived the test, and I learned how to forgive with an open heart."

Karmic Replays with New Players

Sometimes a karmic replay happens with the same person, as in Bobbi's case. Bobbi and George were given another chance to be together in positive circumstances. Sometimes present circumstances are parallel to a past life, but they include different people, as in Sue Ellen's case. She didn't share a past life with her current husband, but a past-life regression helped her break free from a destructive pattern rooted in a karmic replay.

It appeared that Sue Ellen had a perfect life. She was a gorgeous brunette, married to a handsome, successful doctor. They lived in a ten-bedroom mansion with a swimming pool and a three-car garage. However, everything was not as rosy as it appeared on the outside. Inside, Sue Ellen was suffering. She came to have a regression because her five-year marriage had deteriorated into abuse and violence. Sue Ellen declared that if she didn't make a change in her situation, she would die.

Her husband, Bob, controlled her life. He made rules about what she could do or could not do. Sue Ellen couldn't go out with friends for she had no money of her own.

When a friend offered to treat Sue Ellen to a movie, Bob took her keys away so she couldn't leave the house. When she tried to meet another friend a week later, Bob gave her a black eye. Friends eventually stopped calling, and Sue Ellen became lonely and depressed. She spent her empty afternoons walking around the mall. It was one of the few activities Bob permitted her to do.

Bob told her over and over again, "You are only here to take care of me and the house. I pay the bills. I'm the boss around here."

"What if I got a job?" she'd retort.

"What could you possibly do? That BA degree of yours is worthless. You have no marketable skills. You can't even type!"

After the fights, he'd try to make up by buying her lavish gifts. But after a while she realized that she was paying too high a price to have expensive perfume, wear designer clothes, and drive a Mercedes.

Bob was away at a conference, so Sue Ellen used the opportunity to seek help. She had read about my workshops in a night school catalogue and called me for an appointment for a regression. She immediately zeroed in on a past life in which she had luscious black hair and honey-colored skin. Rows of silver bracelets adorned her arms. She wore golden slippers with turned-up toes and a brightly colored dress bejeweled with metal bells that tinkled when she moved.

With a giant grin on her face, Sue Ellen said, "I feel so spoiled and happy. I am so well taken care of. My name is Mina."

She knew that she was a courtesan in the Middle East somewhere, thousands of years ago. She belonged to a very powerful, high-ranking politician. He was sitting on a raised marble throne in a tremendously large hall with archways and columns.

Her heart began to pound as she felt a rush of rage and fear. She and the man were arguing. She knew that they had had this fight before, and that there was no way that she could win.

Sue Ellen was nearly hysterical. She stammered. "What I want doesn't matter. I have no rights, for he owns me. I have fallen in love with another man, and I want to renounce my vows. I am on my knees begging him to set me free, but he won't let me go."

She began sobbing as she recalled being stabbed through the heart as she tried to escape from the thugs the politician had paid to murder her. She filled her wounded heart with an image of a monarch butterfly. We affirmed that she was free to love.

As Sue Ellen came out of her trance, she seemed bewildered. "It's almost a parallel to my marriage to Bob, which has been a struggle between freedom and dependency. The first few years of marriage, I actually believed my role was to do domestic chores and be available for sex with Bob whenever he wanted it. Of course, that was Mina's role as well. She was provided for, and all she had to do was be a concubine.

"It did not occur to me until now that I have allowed myself to be bought and owned. Mina ran away, then was hunted down and murdered. I realized that I have been subconsciously afraid that this would happen to me again. If I left, I would die. Every time I left Bob, I could never go through with a divorce, even after the repeated attacks. Something always held me back.

"I am as beautiful, intelligent, and strong as Mina. I must believe that leaving this marriage will bring me a new life. I don't need someone to buy me things. In order to have an equal relationship, I must give up this need to be kept."

And that's what Sue Ellen did! She went into therapy and divorced her husband. It was difficult, and at times she didn't know if she would have the strength to go through with it. But she persevered and began a new life.

Karmic Replay Issues Exercise

To discover whether you have karmic replay issues, ask yourself the following questions:

- Are you in an abusive relationship, yet don't seek help?
- Do you find yourself asking, "What did I ever do to deserve this?"
- Do you feel that certain relationships are tests?
- Do you feel like you owe something to someone, yet are unsure of why you have that feeling?
- Do you feel like you've been in your present situation before?
- Has your need for security become a prison?
- What part of your life has become so comfortable that it's stagnated?
- What behaviors do you display that seem childish or inappropriate, yet you continue to react that way?

Replay Tarot Visualization

This visualization is designed to help you release an unwanted attachment. It could be an addiction to a person or a situation.

You'll need to use the Rider-Waite deck of tarot cards that you used in chapter 1.

Go to your sacred space. State your intention for this meditation. What do you want to release?

Go through the deck and find the Devil card, number fifteen. Sit upright in a chair, with your spine straight, and place the card on a table in front of you. Focus on the card. Take in the whole image—the colors, the figures, the devil, and the blackness of the background.

This card embodies the archetypal energy of Pan, who is half man, half goat. He is the god of merriment and sensuality. One of the most effective ways to change our consciousness is to see the absurd in life. When we take our problems too seriously, they can ensnare us. When your life looks like the Devil card, laughter can be your greatest aid.

If you currently identify with this card, it means you've lost your sense of humor. You need to get it back, quickly! Make it your priority. Do the following:

- Try renting comedies until you've turned around your frame of mind.
- Listen to laughter meditation CDs by laugh master Laraaji Nadananda from http://dwij.org/rising_stars/laraaji.html.
- Exaggerate your problem. Imagine it twenty times worse. Now imagine it a hundred times worse.
- Imagine everyone you talk to having your problem. Imagine everyone in the world having it!
- Imagine still having your problem when you die.
- Ask the devil to help you find ten other ways to lighten your attachment.
- Laugh until your inner world mirrors your outer mirth.

Karmic Replay Affirmations
Select one of the following affirmations or make up one of your own to help reinforce your karmic replay healing:

- I surrender my life to the higher power that knows what is best for me.
- I am willing to be joyful.

- I retain my sense of humor.
- I handle my problems realistically and mirthfully.
- My life is in divine order.

Karmic Replay Flower Essences

Try working with one or more of these flower essences to support your healing process:

- **Hound's tongue:** restores a sense of wonder and reverence for life
- **Peppermint:** develops a lightness in one's thinking
- **Blackberry:** transforms ideas into action
- **Baby blue eyes:** restores trust in the divine despite harsh experiences
- **Larch:** illuminates mistakes as learning lessons
- **Mustard:** transforms depression into joy
- **Zinnia:** affords a childlike sense of humor
- **Cayenne:** mobilizes one into action

Karmic Shadows

If you have a pattern of attracting romantic partners who all seem to have the same issue, you may be trying to heal a past-life problem. For instance, if you keep getting involved with men or women who are unable to commit to you, there may be something about that issue from a past life that you didn't integrate in a past life. Any time you catch yourself blaming others for your problems, you are dealing with a *karmic shadow*.

Karmic shadows help you get in touch with a part of yourself that has been kept in the dark. You are challenged to look at areas where you are not being responsible. It may appear to be someone else who has the problem, when actually it is you.

For instance, Laura wanted a family. She had been living with her boyfriend, Tom, for three years. When she talked about getting married, Tom said he wasn't ready. A year later, when she turned twenty-nine, she brought up the subject of marriage again. Once again, Tom couldn't make a commitment. Laura wasn't content to be strung along, so she left him.

Now she was in her mid-thirties, and once again she was involved with a man who wouldn't slip the diamond ring on her finger. Her biological clock was ticking, and her desperation led her to have a regression with me to understand her block.

Laura asked me to give her reiki while she was being hypnotized. When I placed my hands on her face, I felt her trembling with fear so I said, "It's totally safe to let go of this."

Her breathing became erratic as she recalled a past life. She said in a panicked voice, "I'm hiding in the bushes on a hillside. Six Indians have come into our homestead. My children are screaming, but I am too paralyzed to move."

Tears were streaming down her face as she continued to remember.

"Oh my God. My house is on fire! The flames are shooting high into the sky. Yet I stay hidden. I know that if they see me, I'll be killed. But my children . . . They are taking my children and our two horses. I have lost everything—my home, family . . ."

I asked her what happened.

While under hypnosis, Laura's body retracted into a fetal position while she was lying on the massage table. She hugged her knees into her chest as she said, "I never recover. When people from the town find me days later, I have gone mad. A widow from the town takes me into her home to care for me, but I die a few days later of a heart attack."

After we transformed the painful memory into love and healing, Laura reclaimed her spirit by filling the hole in her heart with

pink light and an image of Kwan Yin, her favorite goddess of compassion. We then affirmed that it was safe for her to love again.

When Laura came out of trance she said, "I was really happy
and in love in that past life. When I lost it, I lost myself. No wonder I've been afraid to have a family!

"Every guy I've dated since high school was never serious
when it came to marriage. I always thought there was something
wrong with them. Now I see that I was the one with the block!
My fear was attracting unavailable partners. In this way, I was
safe. If you don't have love, you can't lose it!"

Karmic Shadows Exercise

If your relationship is unsatisfying and you tend to find fault
with your partner, try answering the following questions:

- Do you get involved with unavailable partners? People
  who are married, have a different sexual orientation, live
  far away, or have different life goals?
- Do you attract the same type of person, knowing that he or
  she isn't really good for you?
- Do you hear yourself saying, "If only *they* would change"?
- Do you blame others for your problems?

If any of these are true, stop and look within. Instead of
blaming other people for not giving you what you want, take
responsibility for your part in your relationships.

Now ask yourself the next questions:

- Why are you creating this situation with your partner?
- What is the payoff from your relationship? What are you
  getting out of it?

If you're feeling blocked, try tapping into your inner guidance
through your dreams. Before going to sleep, ask your higher self

to reveal an insight about your karmic shadow. Keep a notebook and pen next to your bed. When you wake up, write down your dreams. Repeat this every night until you receive an answer.

Frozen Moments Meditation

This meditation is another way to access past-life memories. It can be very effective for those who have strong clairsentient abilities. Before you start, mentally state your intention for the session. What do you want to accomplish?

Go to your sacred space. Choose some music to play that inspires you to move your body, and put it on before you begin this meditation. You may want to record the following script and play it along with the music. Make sure to pause after each suggestion. Allow about twenty minutes to complete the whole meditation.

Lie on your back and close your eyes. Take a few deep breaths. Feel where your body connects to the floor. Allow yourself to sink deeper into the floor. Focus on your breath. With each breath, you melt even deeper into the floor.

Begin to stretch your body. Move into different positions that feel good. Whatever you may be feeling, express it through a movement. If you feel heavy, you may want to stamp your feet or to sway your arms like an elephant's trunk.

Keep your eyes closed as you come to a standing position. Focus on your body as you take tiny steps. Try spinning in a circle. Create your own dance. Just let go. Allow yourself to express each part of your body. If you feel light, surrender to playful movements. Sway your hips. You may want to crawl like a baby, roll and tumble, or jump up and down.

Let yourself feel like a child again. Joyfully bend and straighten your knees. Wiggle your toes. Swim through the air with your arms. Scrunch up your face. Allow the movement to carry you away.

Freeze your body into a position. What shape is the outline of your body forming? If you were a statue, what would you look like? Are you male or female? What kind of gesture are you making? If you were an actor, what kind of character would you be playing? What kind of scene would you be performing in? Is your character starring in a drama or a comedy? Are you engaging in an action scene? Notice whether any emotions are coming to the surface. Trust the information you receive. Hold your pose for as long as you like.

When you are ready, slowly open your eyes.

Write about your experience in your journal. Record any impressions that you did receive. You may want to use colored pens to draw shapes or images that you saw. Don't be discouraged if you feel that you didn't get any past-life information. This exercise will help you use your right brain, which is creative and intuitive. With practice, you will be able to access soul wisdom with ease.

Karmic Shadow Affirmations
Select one of the following affirmations, or make up your own to enhance your karmic shadow healing:

- I am open to receive guidance from my higher self.
- I trust in the divine power that gives me support.
- I receive guidance from my dreams.

Karmic Shadow Flower Essences
Try one of the following flower essences to enhance your inner guidance:

- **Black-eyed Susan:** encourages emotional honesty with oneself
- **Angelica:** enhances receptivity to spiritual guidance in dreams

- **Mugwort:** expands awareness while in the dream state
- **Star tulip:** enhances awareness of the symbols in dreams
- **Dandelion:** releases tension stored in the body
- **Snapdragon:** contacts core emotions

Karmic Flip-Flops

Over the years I've found another interesting pattern that many people experience while undergoing a past-life regression. It is a kind of role reversal. You may have been in a relationship with someone in a past life and then discover that your roles in this life are reversed. If you were a woman in a past life, you may be a man in this life, or vice versa. Or you may be the same sex now.

Your circumstances may also be inverted in this life. Usually you are both working to heal a previous life where there was unequal power in the relationship. As a result, one person suffered. Being in the other person's shoes helps you to balance the scales. I call these role reversal relationships *karmic flip-flops*.

Kelly was divorced and a grandmother. She began exploring past lives to gain more insight into her long-distance relationship with her lover, Steve. Their attraction was so passionate they felt addicted to each other; their fervor was hard to explain.

When they first met eight years ago, they both felt as if they already knew each other. After two months of a whirlwind romance, he went home to his farm in Delaware while she stayed on in her townhouse in New York. Steve called her nearly every day for a month, and then he disappeared from her life.

Steve didn't have a cell phone, voice mail, or email, so Kelly couldn't reach him. She let his home phone ring and ring, at all times of the day and night, but there was never any answer.

Then, when Kelly had given up on ever seeing him again, he reappeared at her door unannounced, six months later. When he arrived, it was as though they had never been apart. They spent a couple of sizzling days together, and then he left without making plans to get together again. That's how it continued over the years. Whenever he walked out the door, Kelly never knew when or whether she'd see him again.

She begged him for a commitment, but Steve was evasive.

"I'm not the marrying kind. I like my freedom."

Steve's unpredictable coming and going was driving her crazy. Kelly felt helpless, for the relationship was out of her control. When she called me for an appointment, I suggested that a regression could help her to resolve her feelings.

In my office, as Kelly relaxed into her past life, she saw that she was a young man with a salt-and-pepper beard, wearing a formal suit. She knew her name was Thomas Handley and that she lived in England.

"I am standing at an altar with a pretty young woman wearing a wedding gown. She has long red, wavy hair and delicate features."

When Kelly recognized the bride as her lover, Steve, she became very happy. With a big smile she said, "It's weird. I'm a man and he's a woman."

I asked Kelly to move to the source of her problem with Steve.

"My wife and I are arguing on a dock. She is upset because I am leaving to work on a project in another city. She hates life in America, because she is separated from her family and friends. She is screaming, 'I hate you! I hate you!'

"This is the recurring problem in my marriage. I always leave her behind for months at a time, feeling angry and alone. I can't understand my wife's feelings. I work hard to provide for her."

I asked Kelly how the problem resolved.

"My wife dies giving birth."

Tears streamed down Kelly's face as she released the painful memory. When she asked her higher self for guidance, her inner voice said, "You need to learn to give love unconditionally to Steve, without wanting something back. Give Steve the freedom that Tom Handley had."

Kelly released her sadness and frustration by imagining that she was letting a white bird fly out of a golden cage.

When Kelly came back to waking awareness she said, "It was so strange seeing our sex roles reversed! But it makes so much sense! Now I know why I always felt that I already knew him. I'm really sorry that I hurt him. I worked all the time, and I left him all alone. I only saw him when it conveniently fit into my schedule."

Two days later, Kelly phoned me. "You'll never believe who showed up out of the blue yesterday."

"Ah, Steve?"

"I haven't seen him for four months. For the first time, I am not feeling anxious now that he's gone. We had a great time and actually talked about our feelings. I finally got it. He isn't going to change. My choice is to accept him for who he is, enjoy him when he's here, and not to expect something from him that he can't give. He can't commit to sharing a day-to-day routine, so he wouldn't make a good husband for me anyway.

"My problem was that I'd be hurt every time he'd leave. I would take his going away as rejection, which it wasn't. Steve loves me. He told me that I'm the most important person in his life. No matter what happens, I'll always love him. But I need to let go."

Karmic Flip-Flop Issues Exercise

To discover whether you have karmic flip-flop issues, ask yourself the following questions:

- Are you in a relationship of unequal power?
- Do you feel you are always giving but don't get anything back in return?

- Is commitment an issue for you or your partner?
- Are you giving your power away to another?
- Do you feel that you need to control another?
- Do you give your partner the freedom he or she needs?
- How does the relationship mirror your self-worth?
- Are you unable to compromise?

Karmic Flip-Flop Tarot Visualization

For this visualization, you'll need to use the Rider-Waite deck of tarot cards that you used in chapter 1. State your intention for this meditation. What do you want to know?

Go through the deck and find the Lovers card, number six. Sit upright in a chair, with your spine straight, and place the card on a table in front of you. Focus on the card. Take in the whole image—the colors, the figures, the angel, and the mountain in the background. Close your eyes and see whether you can recall the card in your mind's eye. Practice this until you can recall the card in detail if you are clairvoyant. Or you may just have a sense of the card if you are clairsentient.

With your eyes closed, imagine the card growing larger and larger, until the figures in it are life-size. Step into the card. Look around you. What time of day is it? What is the weather like? How does the air feel against your skin? Do you hear any sounds? Do you notice any smells?

Now approach the female figure. She has an important message to tell you regarding the feminine role in your relationship. Receive the message now. Let it flow into your mind.

Now approach the male figure. He has an important message to tell you regarding the male role in your relationship. Receive the message now. Let it flow into your mind.

Now approach the angel. Feel him radiating unconditional love to you. You feel a sense of awe to be in the presence of such a being. The angel has a gift for you, something that you can take back into your life. This will heal your relationship. Accept the gift and study it carefully. What is it? Ask how you can use it. The answer flows into your mind. Thank the angel and the lovers. Take one last look around, then step out of the card. When you are out, the card shrinks back to its normal size. When you are ready, slowly open your eyes.

Write the answers to the following questions in your journal:

- What time of day was it?
- What was the weather like?
- Did you hear any sounds?
- Did you notice any smells?
- What message did the female figure have for you?
- What message did the male figure have for you?
- What was the gift you received from the angel?
- How are you to use it?
- Did you notice or experience anything else?

Karmic Flip-Flop Affirmations

Select one of the following affirmations or make up your own to enhance your healing:

- I stop making my partner wrong.
- I am equal to my partner, and he or she is equal to me.
- I am honest with myself and others.
- I allow others to be powerful.
- I am happy with myself whether I have a mate or not.
- I win, everyone wins.

Karmic Flip-Flop Flower Essences

Try one of the following flower essence to help heal your karmic flip-flop issues:

- **Black cohosh:** heals power struggles in relationships
- **Vine:** releases the need to dominate another person
- **Fairy lantern:** releases the need to give away your power to another person
- **Centaury:** helps you resist exploitive relationships
- **Chicory:** releases the need to manipulate others

conclusion

Congratulations! I want to acknowledge you for the extraordinary person that you are and for embarking on a journey of self-discovery. It takes courage to delve into the unknown. You have to be willing to confront your fears, clean up your mistakes, claim ultimate responsibility for your life and actions, and give up blaming others. Karmic healing is some of the most difficult yet most rewarding and important work that you can do. When you understand who and what you are, you can respond to life events with true awareness. You stop taking things personally and reacting out of insecurity, fear, and anger and respond to events and others with open-hearted compassion. You are at peace—within and without.

As we close, go to your sacred space so you can accept and acknowledge your accomplishments. Set the stage for going within to get in touch and get true answers by lighting a candle or burning some incense. Center yourself and take a few deep breaths. Answer the following questions.

- What goals did you achieve?
- Which relationships healed?
- What aspects of your life have healed?
- How has your family life improved?
- How has your health improved?
- Has your professional life improved?
- Are you more relaxed?
- Is it easier to concentrate?
- Do you feel more peaceful?
- What areas need more work?
- What new projects are you undertaking?
- What's next?

Wherever you are on your healing journey is perfect. Some of you may need more time to complete your karmic healing. Some may need to go back and practice some of the healing exercises and meditations. Sometimes an old issue reappears, and now you can view it with a new perspective. Be patient with yourself.

If you continue to practice the principles of karmic healing, your personal power will increase, and you are apt to make better choices. When you clear the static of your racing mind, you are more in touch with what your soul really yearns to experience—that we are all one. We all want to participate in co-creating a world where everyone lives together in harmony with nature and each other.

Growth is a cyclical process. If you observe nature, you'll see that life travels in cycles and seasons. Every day, the sun comes up in the morning and sets in the evening. Each month, the moon waxes across the sky into fullness and then wanes back to darkness. Spring turns into summer, summer moves into autumn and then into winter and back to spring. The universe is constantly in a state of life, death, and renewal, just as you are always transforming.

When you are no longer bound to past karmic scripts, you are free to create a future of your dreams. So I invite you to reinvent your life, like an artist standing in front of a blank canvas. You now hold a palette of all the karmic healing colors. What kind of future do you want to paint for yourself? What inspires you? Who do you want to become? How can you make the world a better place?

I'd love to hear about all of your miracles and breakthroughs, so please feel free to share them with me at my website, www.djunaverse.com.

Karmic Dictionary

Aura: The electromagnetic energy that surrounds your physical body and connects you energetically to dimensions beyond the physical dimension.

Autopilot: Your automatic response system that is built into your subconscious from your habits and repetitive behavior.

Blockage: Thoughts and unexpressed emotions connected to unresolved issues that are held in our body's cells and perceived as tension, stiffness, or pain.

Body baggage: Physical symptoms remaining in your body's cellular memory from past lives that affect your present health.

Fate filters: Decisions made in past lives that limit your current beliefs and subsequent actions.

Feng shui: An ancient Chinese healing practice of aligning the life force energy of your home with the energy flow of the earth.

Guilt quilts: Emotional remnants carried over from past lives that function as false security blankets, covering true feelings and masking potentially positive choices.

Higher self: Your soul awareness, which is both eternal and divine, and knows your true purpose.

Interlife: A nonphysical dimension that is in between incarnations, where you have access to your soul's wisdom.

Karmic alarm: Your intuition alerting you to danger.

Karmic carryovers: Unsettled scores from past lives characterized by hate, rage, anger, and/or a desire for revenge.

Karmic catalyst: Relationships that present painful lessons that force you to grow. It's like being in a karmic boot camp. You are trained to become stronger.

Karmic clashes: Interactions with people who have very different beliefs from yours and expand your vision of the world.

Karmic clinkers: People who illustrate a negative quality in you, which motivates you to grow in the opposite way.

Karmic cloaks: Relationships or circumstances that present painful lessons. At the time, it's very hard to see anything positive is to be gained from your involvement; the potential for growth is concealed.

Karmic clock: Your built-in timing mechanism that determines when you will deal with a karmic issue.

Karmic clog: An unresolved soul issue that creates a blockage in your aura, which can manifest as a health problem, fear, or limitation.

Karmic clutter: Anything you have outgrown but continue to hang on to that acts as a block to your growth.

Karmic coaches: Especially close relationships that help you through a crisis and/or affirm your positive attributes.

Karmic connection: When the root cause of your problem is revealed.

Karmic costume: The biological karma you inherit from your family. This includes your physical, emotional, and mental patterns.

Karmic crossroad: When you become aware that you have a problem; you have the freedom to face it and solve it, or ignore it and stay stuck.

Karmic detectors: Clues that help you notice or discover karmic issues.

Karmic flip-flops: Relationships that are role reversals. Both of you are working to heal a previous life where there was unequal power in the relationship. As a result, one person suffered. Being placed in the other person's shoes helps you to balance the scales.

Karmic healing: When a karmic clog is released, you are free of the karmic carryover that controlled your unconscious behavior. You are then free to make better choices in your life.

Karmic intermission: The time between lives when you plan your soul lessons and soul contracts with family members and other relations.

Karmic pattern: Destructive behavior that is repeated through many incarnations.

Karmic pop-ups: Irrational emotions and responses that seem to surface out of context, unpredictably. They are your soul's way of getting you to pay attention.

Karmic red flags: Relationships in which hazardous conditions exist; exercise caution in these relationships for they are truly treacherous.

Karmic replays: Situations that you also experienced in a past life. The people's names may have changed, but it's the same setup. You didn't learn the first time, so here's another chance.

Karmic revenge: Giving a problem up to the higher power and letting the law of karma balance the scales, instead of trying to get even.

Karmic shadows: Relationships that help you get in touch with a part of yourself that has been kept in the dark. Whether a person or a situation, they help you see where you are not being responsible

Karmic triggers: An outside stimuli that activates a past memory or soul issue, so that you become aware of it and can release it.

Karmic values: Values you hold when you don't know what is truly important; you've outgrown certain values you've inherited from childhood but haven't yet discovered what you really want.

Law of karma: You reap what you sow.

Meditation: Emptying the mind of thoughts to go into a trance state.

Negative pattern: Repeating destructive behavior, without realizing you are caught in a negative cycle.

Ohm: A sacred syllable chanted in Hindu and Buddhist prayers to bring peace, centeredness, and connection to all that is.

Past-life regression therapy: The use of hypnosis to discover the original, past-life causes—real or symbolic—of a present issue or problem.

Positive pattern: Repeating good deeds and healthy habits without awareness of acting in the spirit of goodwill.

Reiki: A hands-on healing technique that channels healing energy to the recipient.

Scale balancers: Extreme actions in other lifetimes that sometimes result in overcompensation in this lifetime.

Visualization: Imagining a desired outcome in your mind's eye.

Recommended Reading and Resources

Ananda Apothecary. http://www.anandaapothecary.com.

The Bach Flower Essences. http://www.bachflower.com.

Bear, Jessica. *Practical Uses and Applications of the Bach Flower Emotional Remedies,* Las Vegas, NV: Balancing Essentials Press, 1993.

Cunningham, Donna, and Andrew Ramer. *The Spiritual Dimensions of Healing Addictions,* San Rafael, CA: Cassandra Press, 1988.

Desert Alchemy Flower Essences. http://www.desert-alchemy.com.

The International Association of Flower Essence Producers. http://floweressenceproducers.org.

International Flower Essence Centre. http://www.flower-essences.com.

Kaminski, Patricia, and Richard Katz. *Flower Essence Repertory: A Comprehensive Guide to North American and English Flower Essences for Emotional and Spiritual Well-Being.* Earth-Spirit, Inc., Box 459, Nevada City, CA, 95959, 800-548-0075.

Scheffer, Mechthild. *Bach Flower Therapy: Theory and Practice.* Rochester, VT: Healing Arts Press, 1988.

index